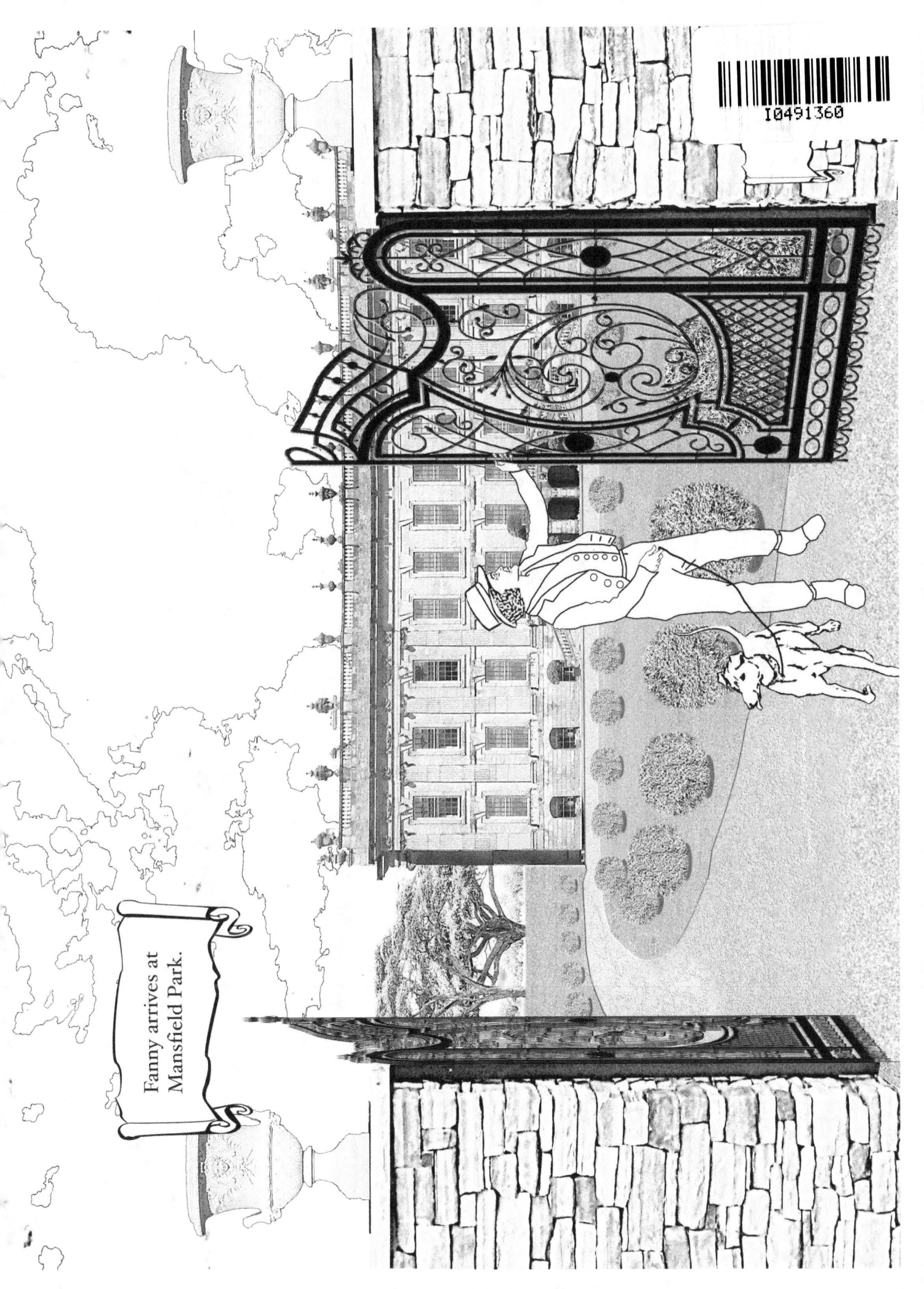

Fanny arrives at Mansfield Park.

I0491360

If you have questions about how to color something, just go to *ucolorclassics.com* and look up the page number. A full size version will show you how Ginny colored it.

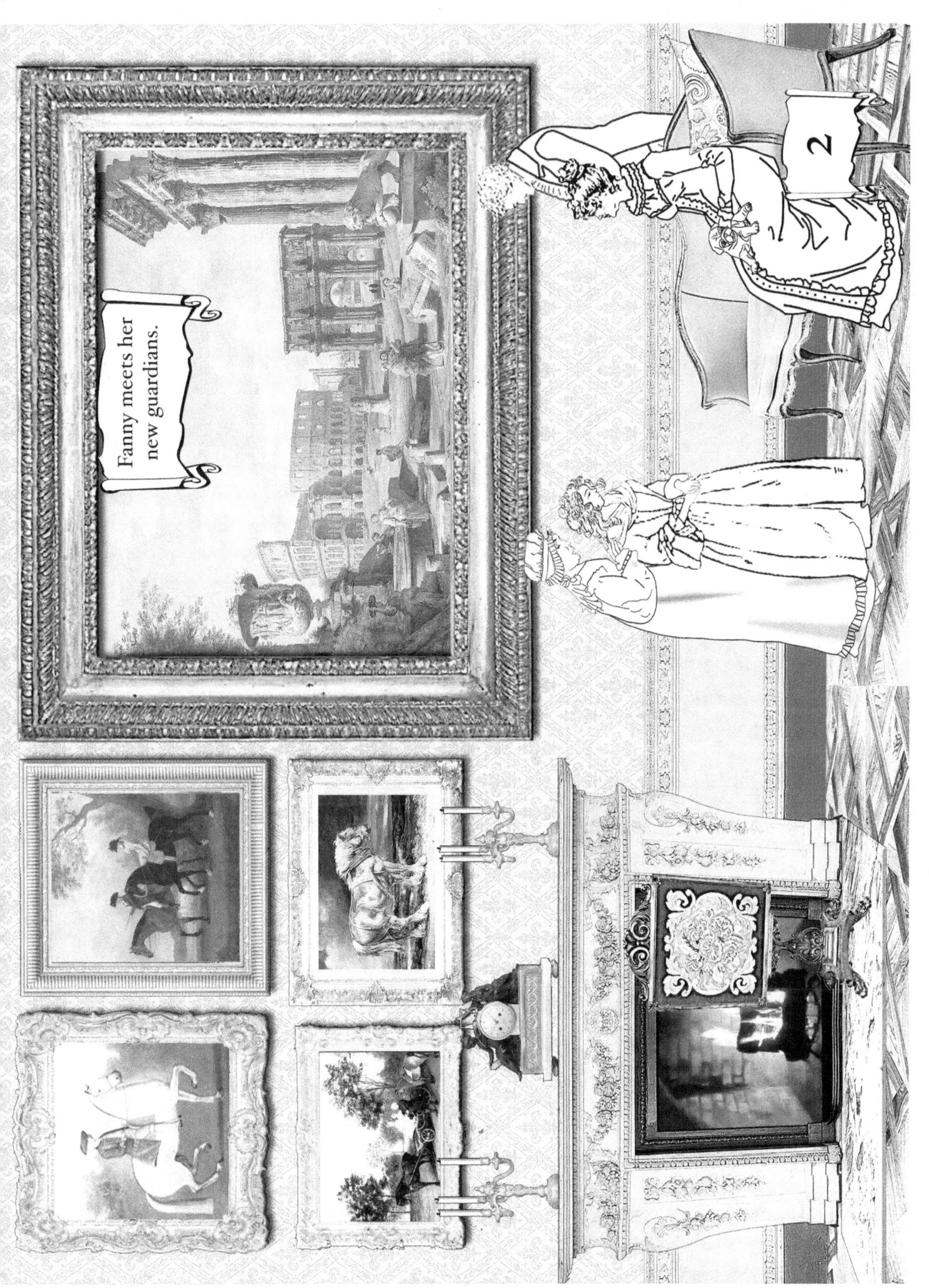

Fanny meets her new guardians.

2

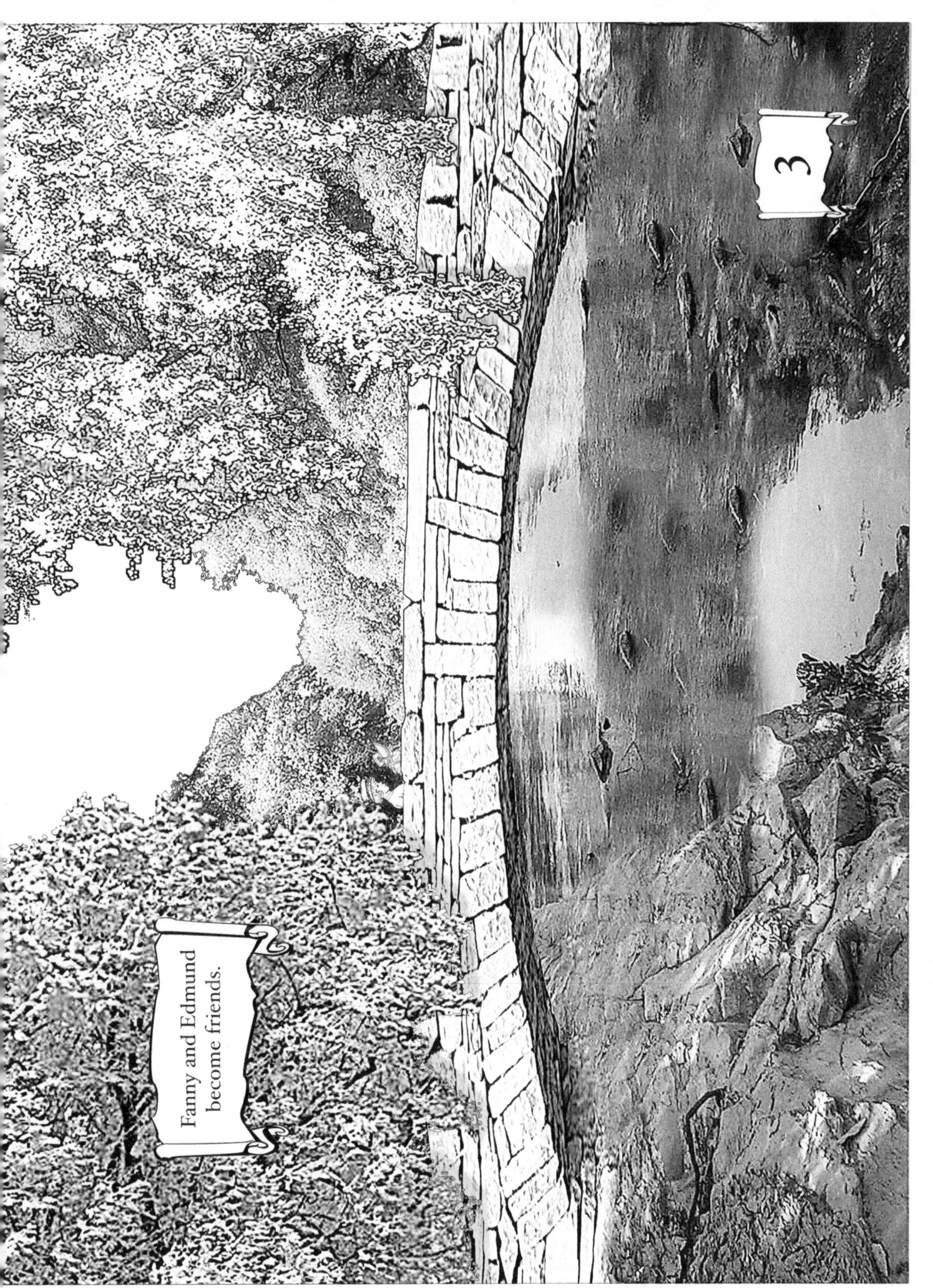

Fanny and Edmund become friends.

3

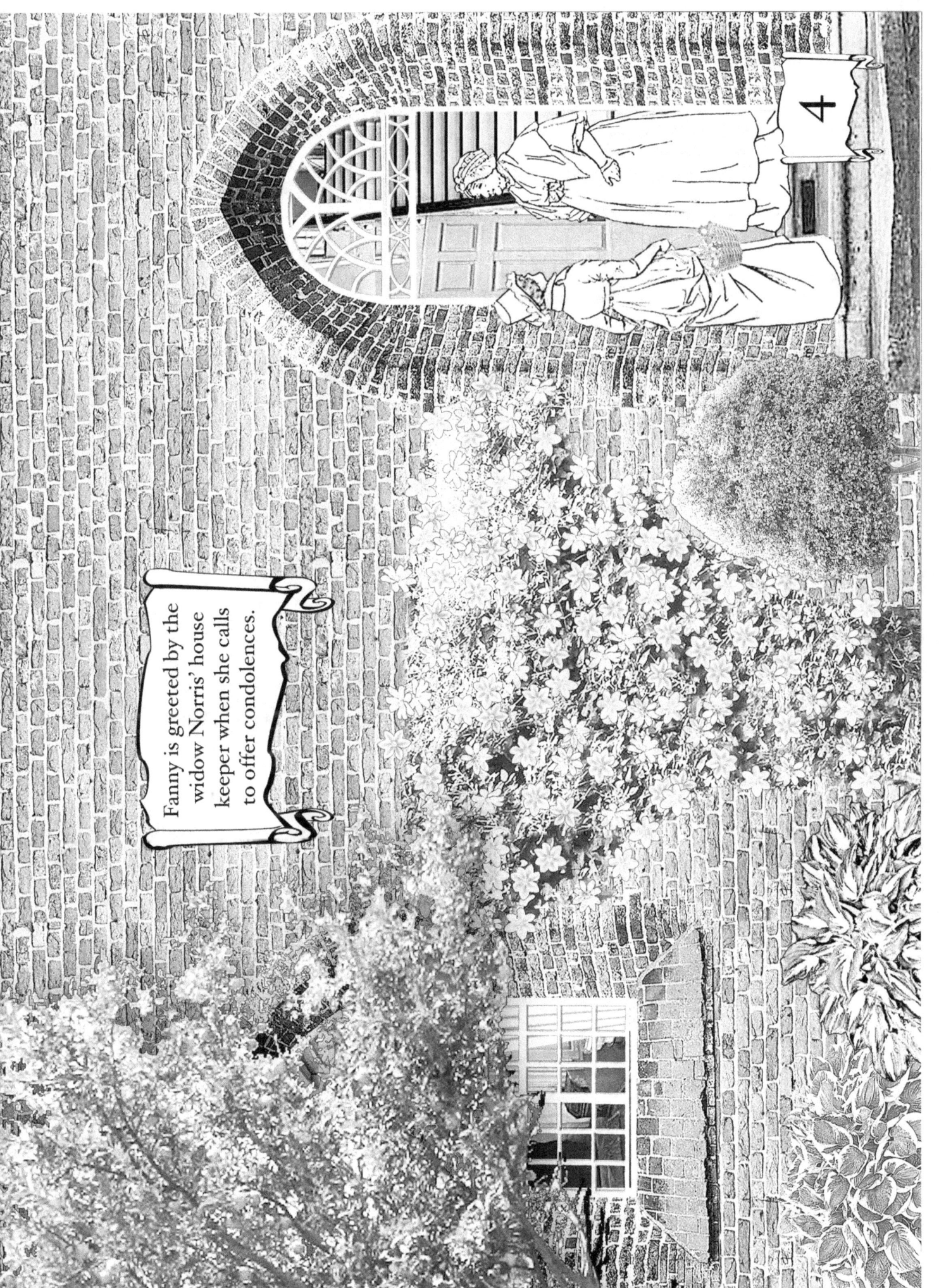

Fanny is greeted by the widow Norris' house keeper when she calls to offer condolences.

4

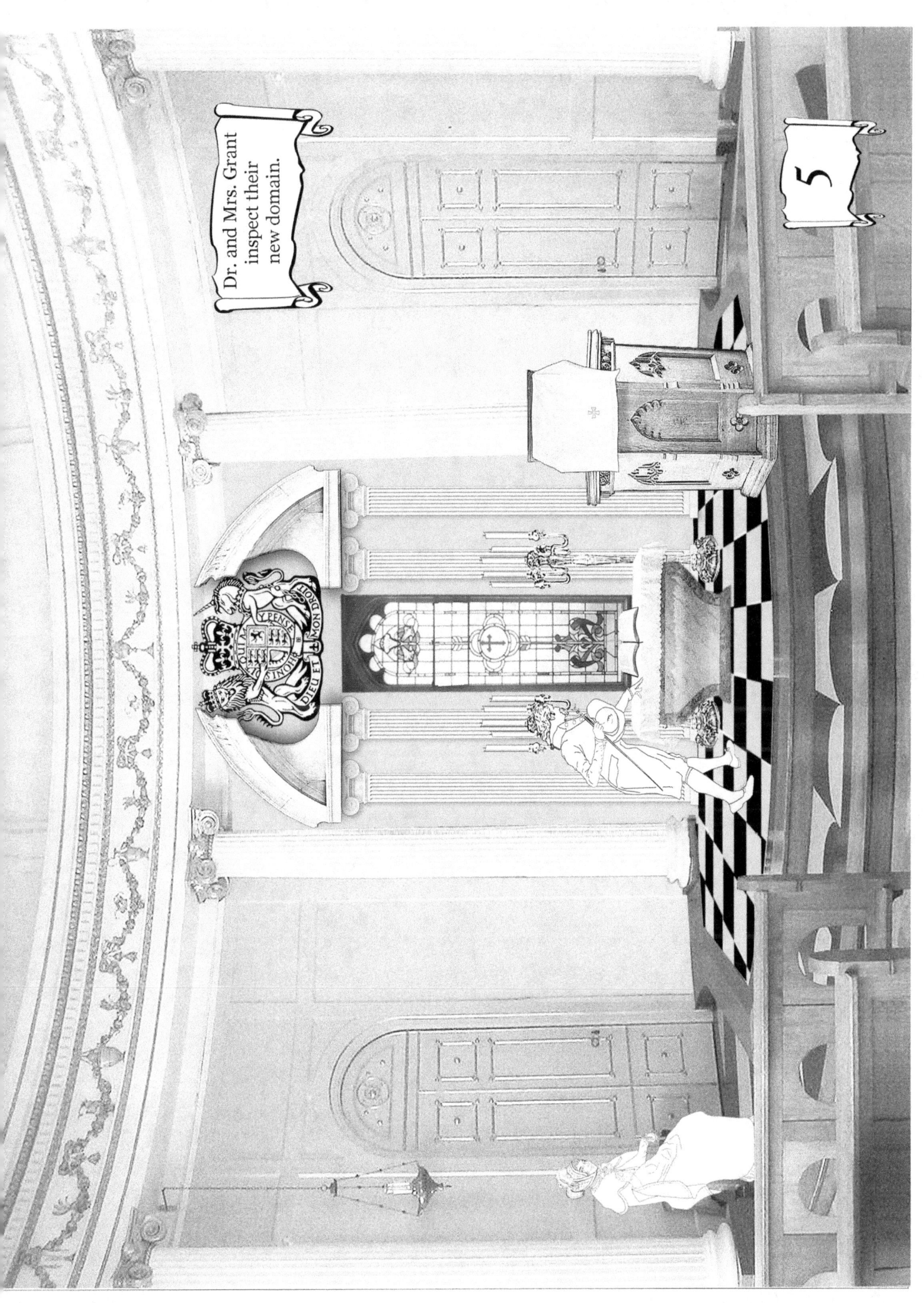

Dr. and Mrs. Grant inspect their new domain.

5

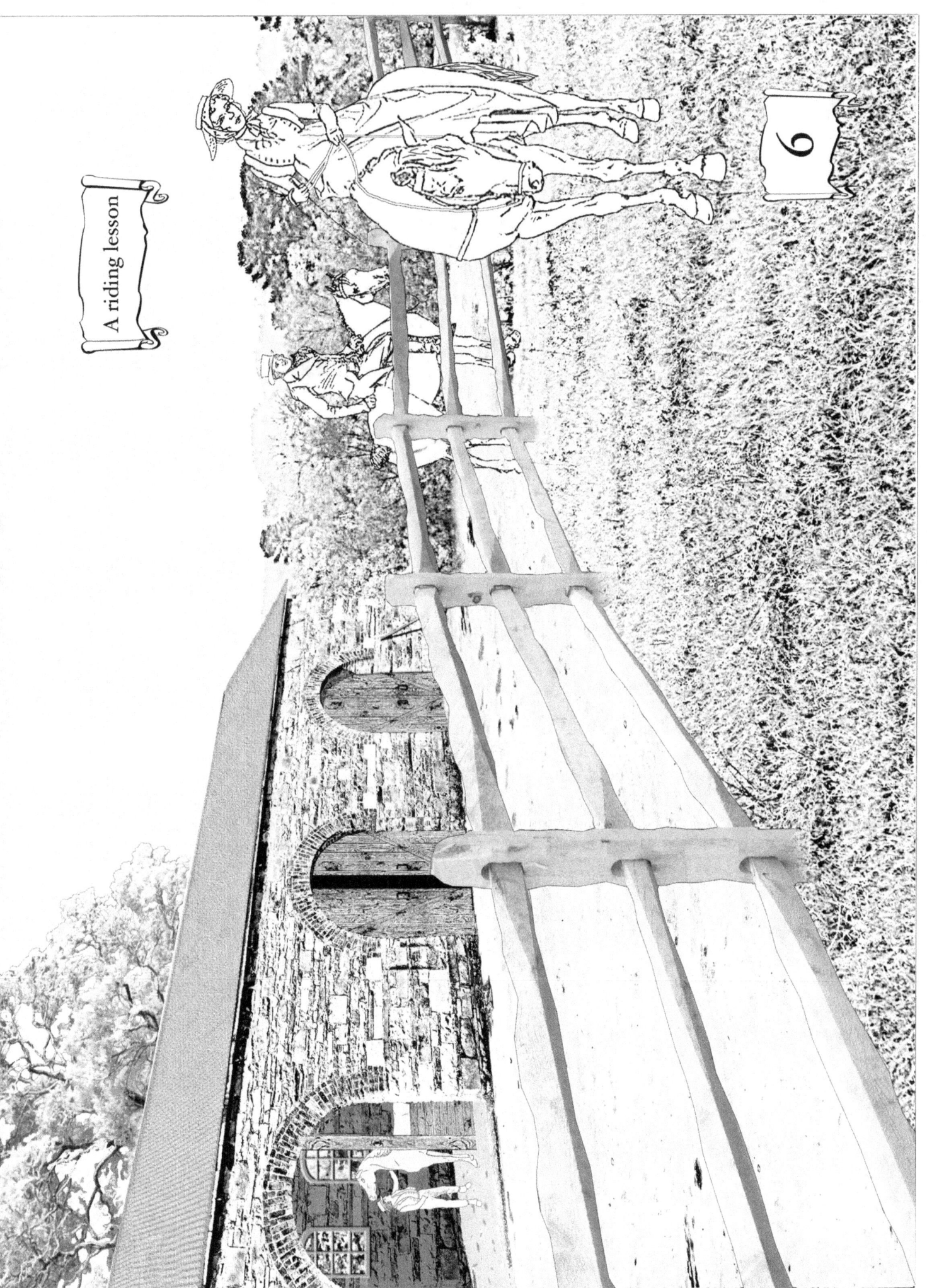

A riding lesson

6

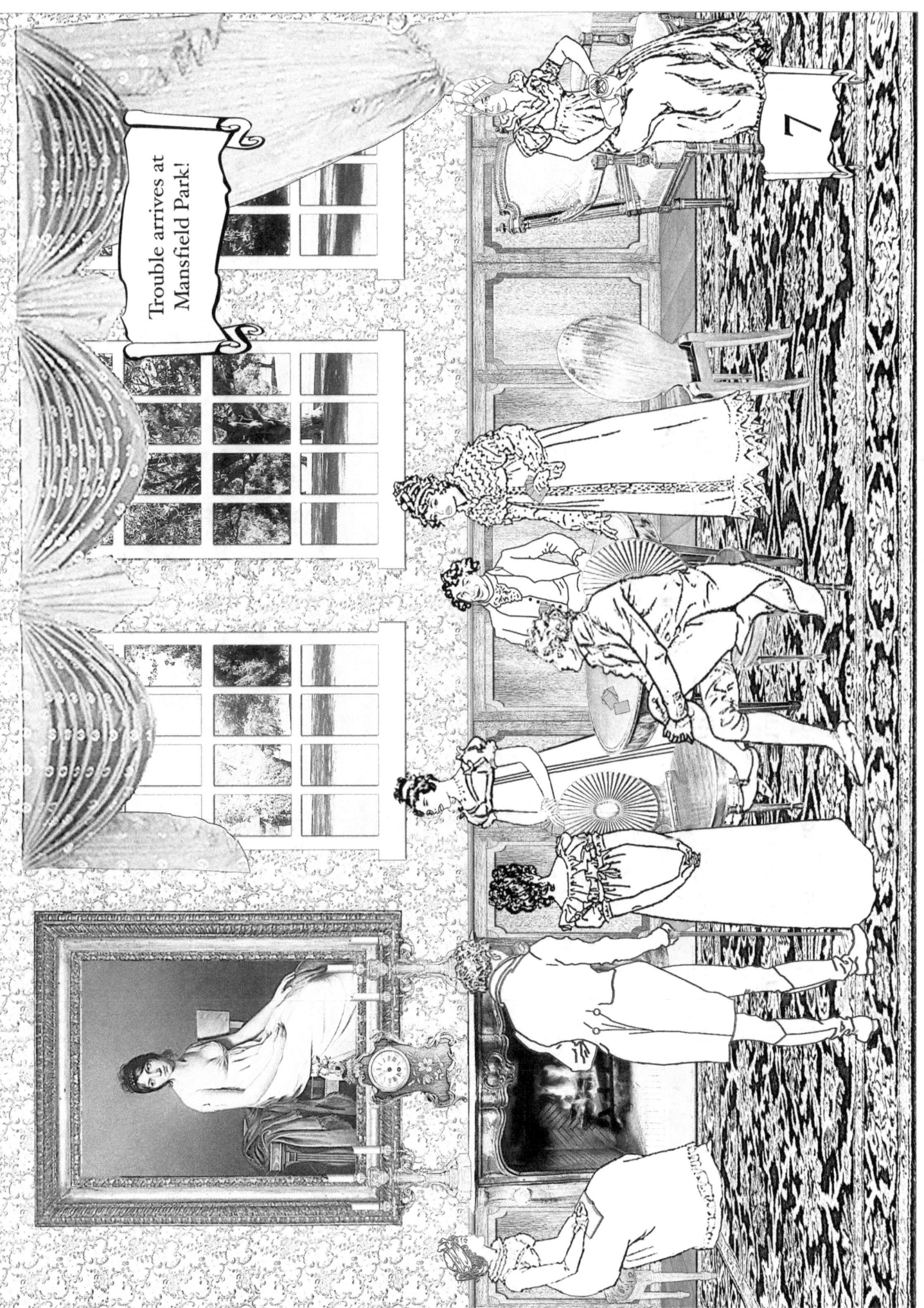

Trouble arrives at Mansfield Park!

7

That metal thing on the floor to the right of the fire is an early oven that had just been recently invented. Its made of brass so color it a shade of yellow.

The things hanging from the ceiling directly over the fireplace are hams and sausages that had been preserved with salt and smoke before being brought into the kitchen.

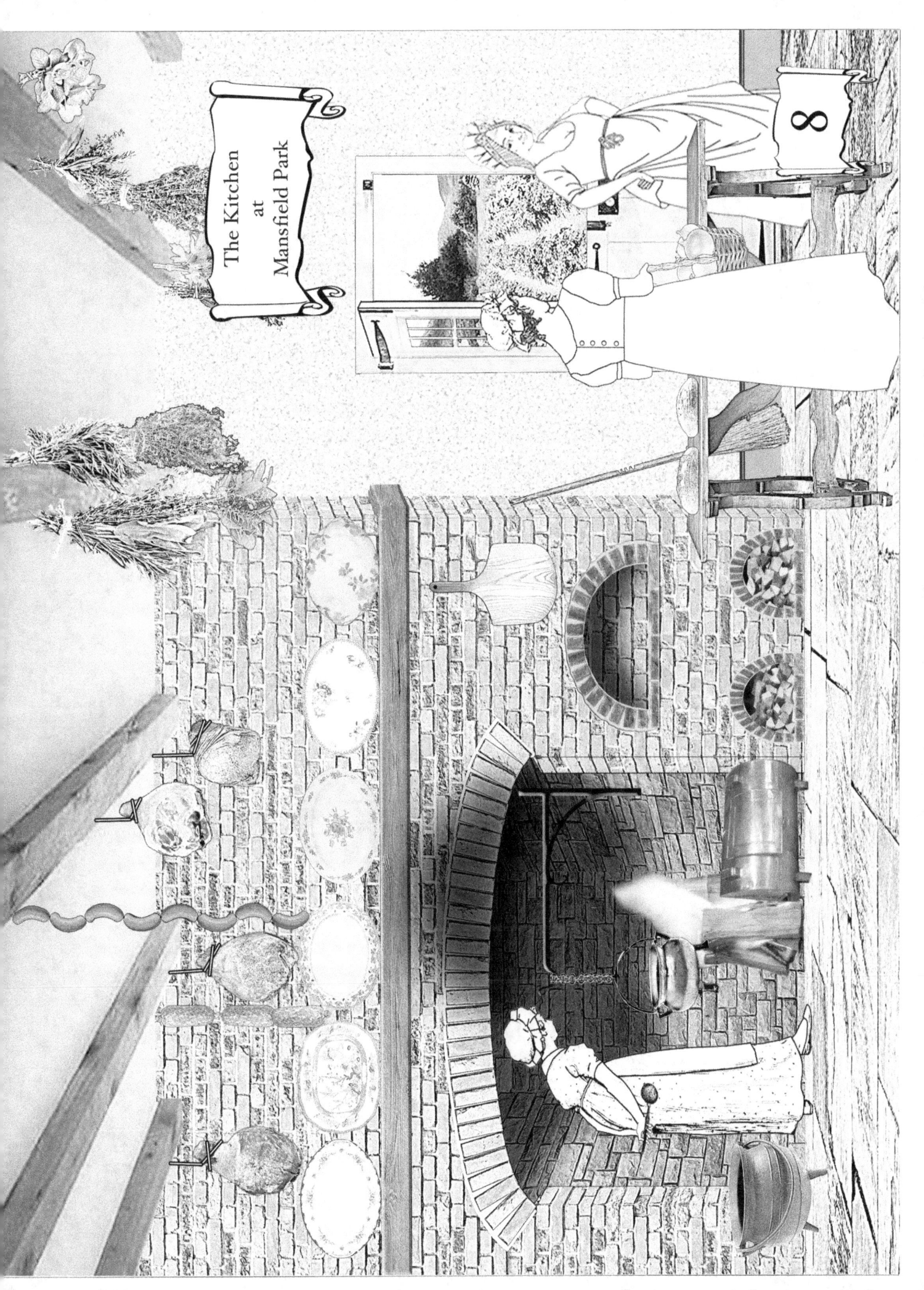

The Kitchen
at
Mansfield Park

8

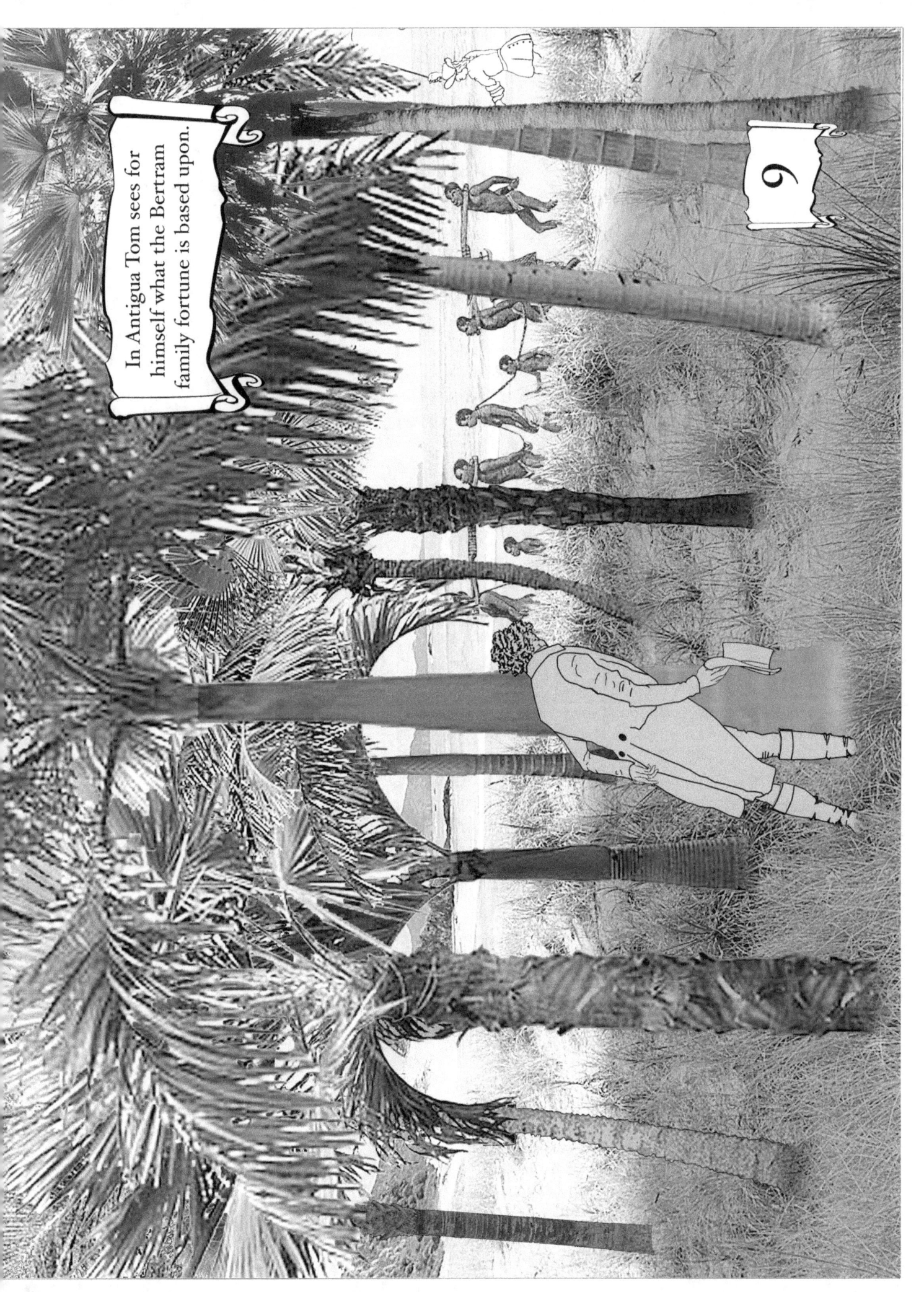

In Antigua Tom sees for himself what the Bertram family fortune is based upon.

9

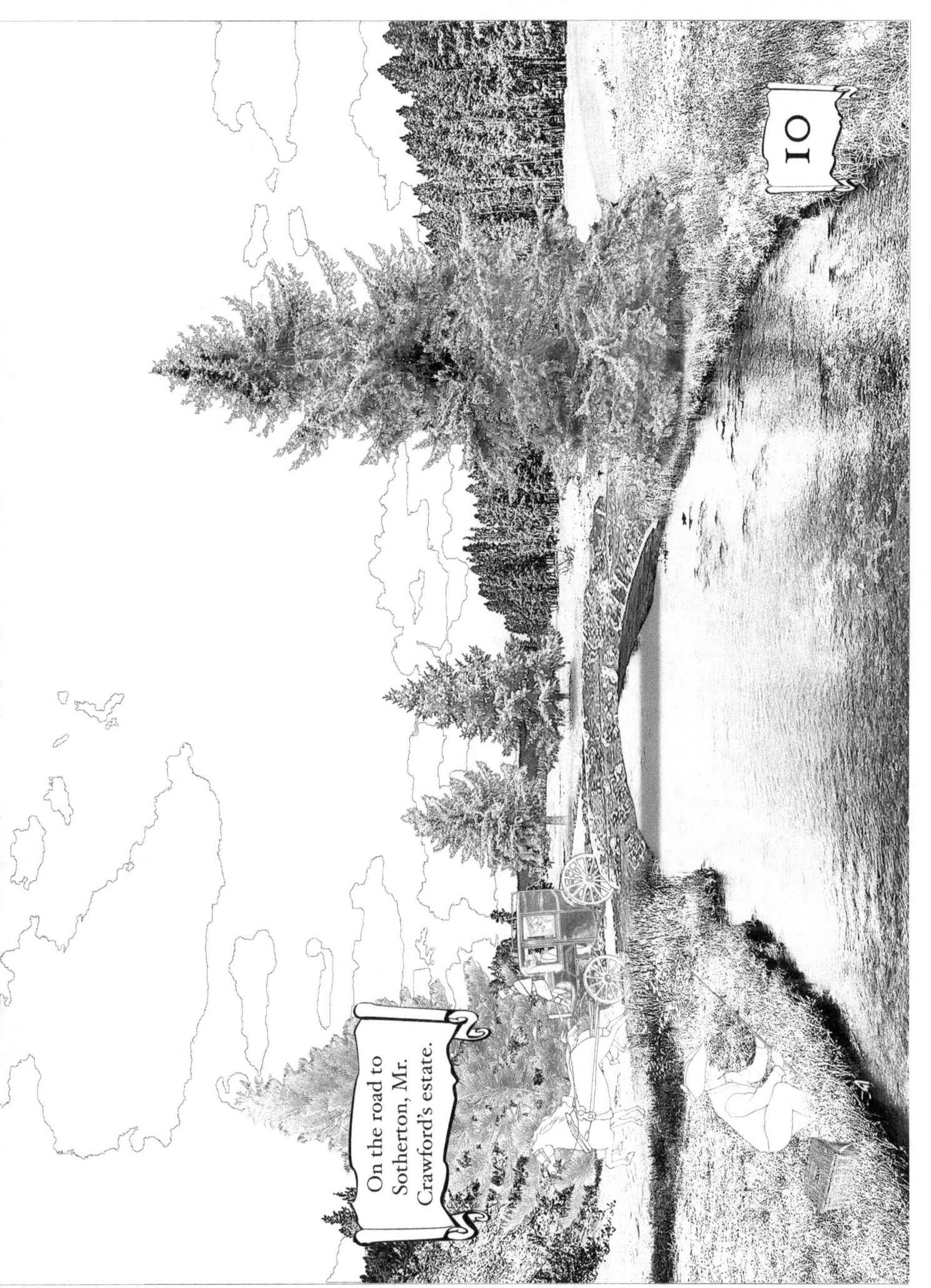

On the road to Sotherton, Mr. Crawford's estate.

IO

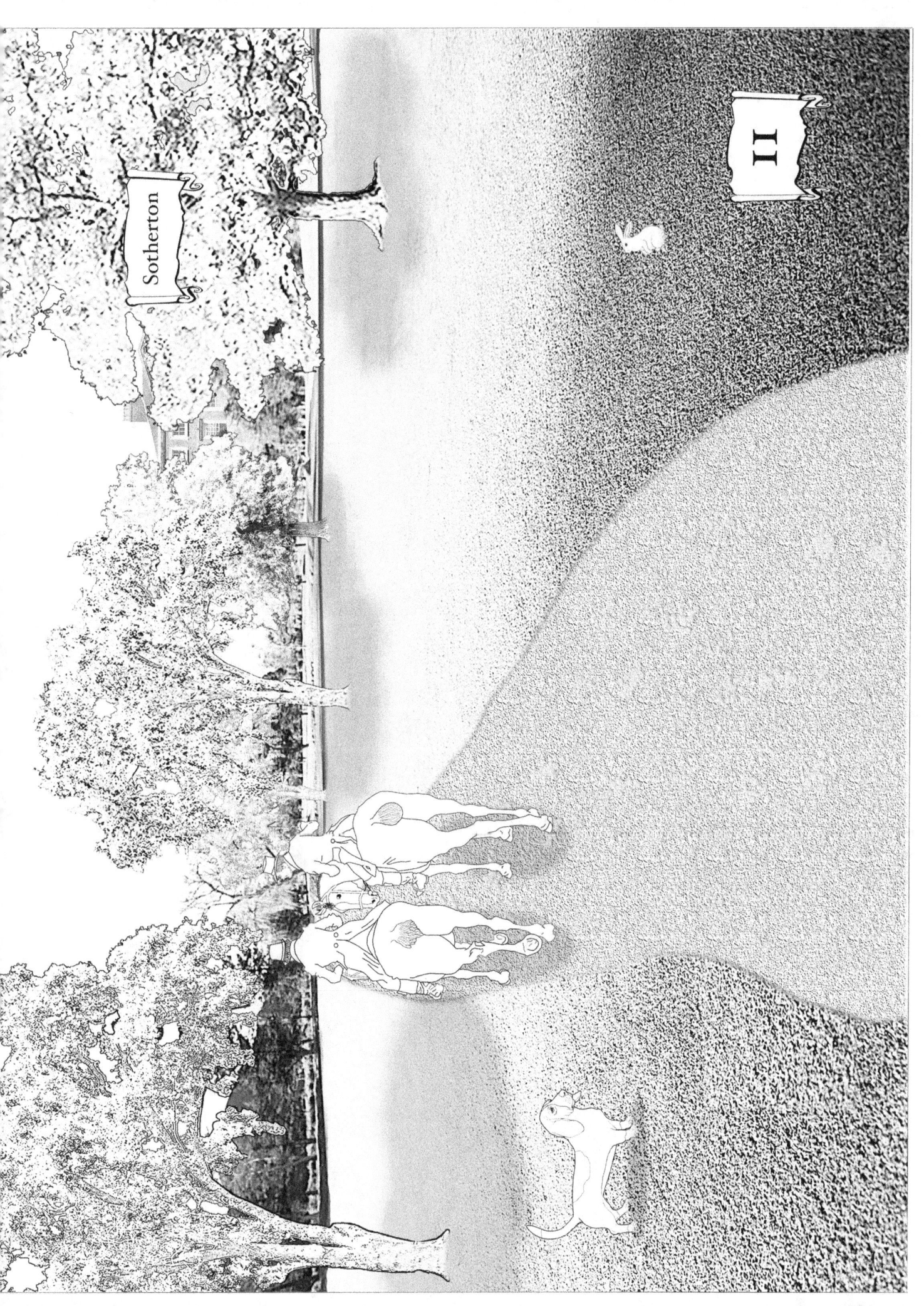

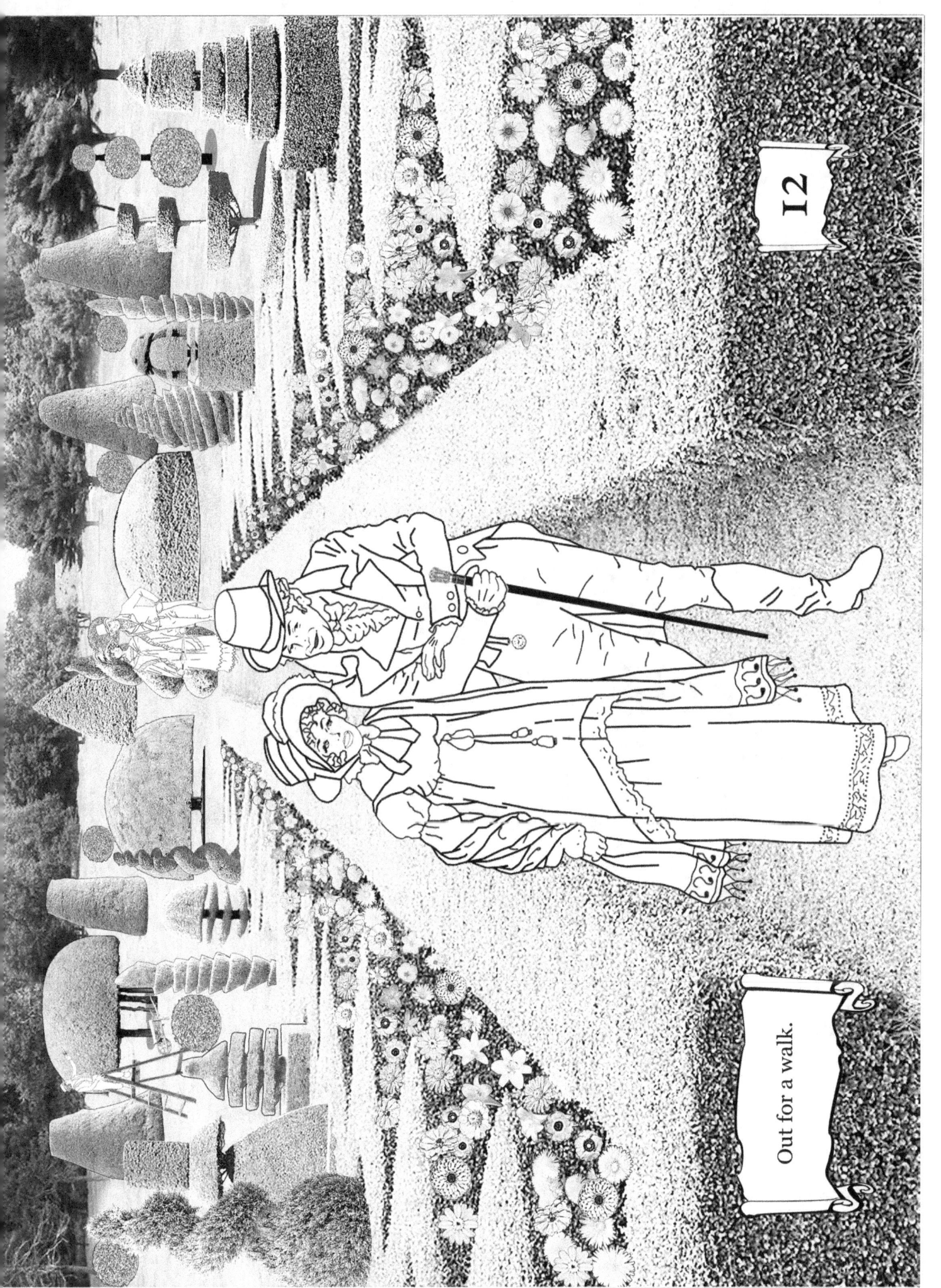

12

Out for a walk.

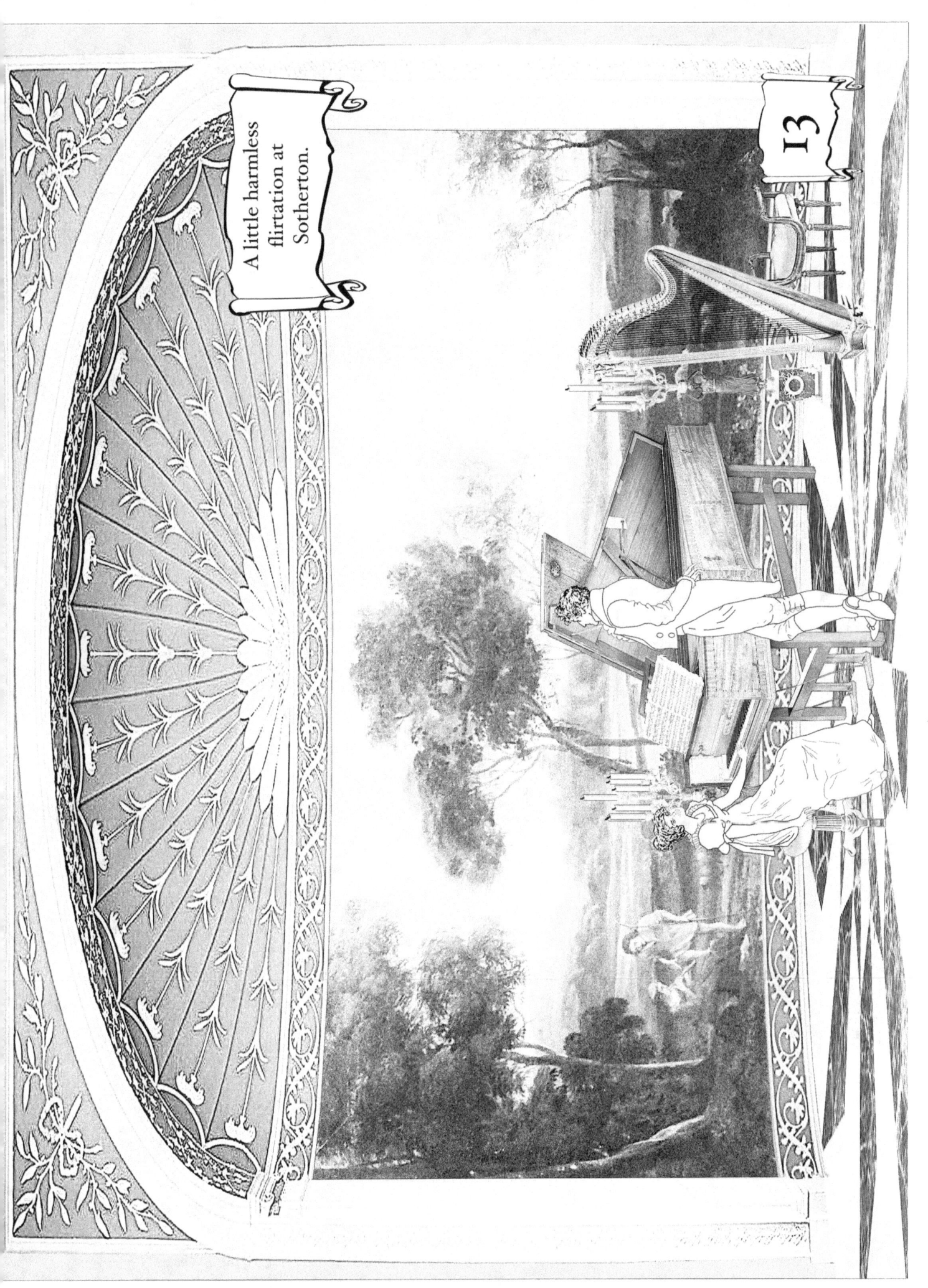

A little harmless flirtation at Sotherton.

13

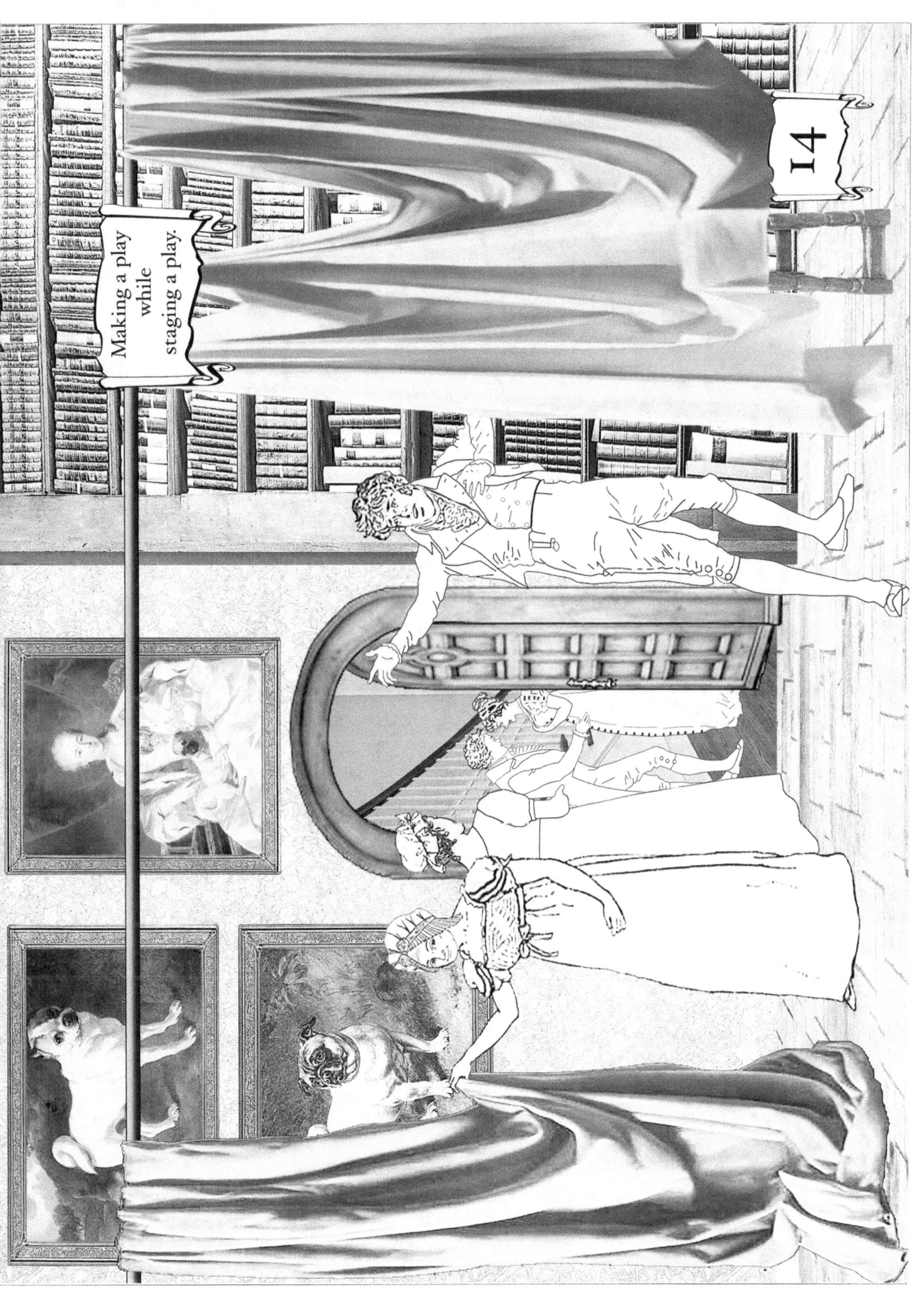

Making a play
while
staging a play.

14

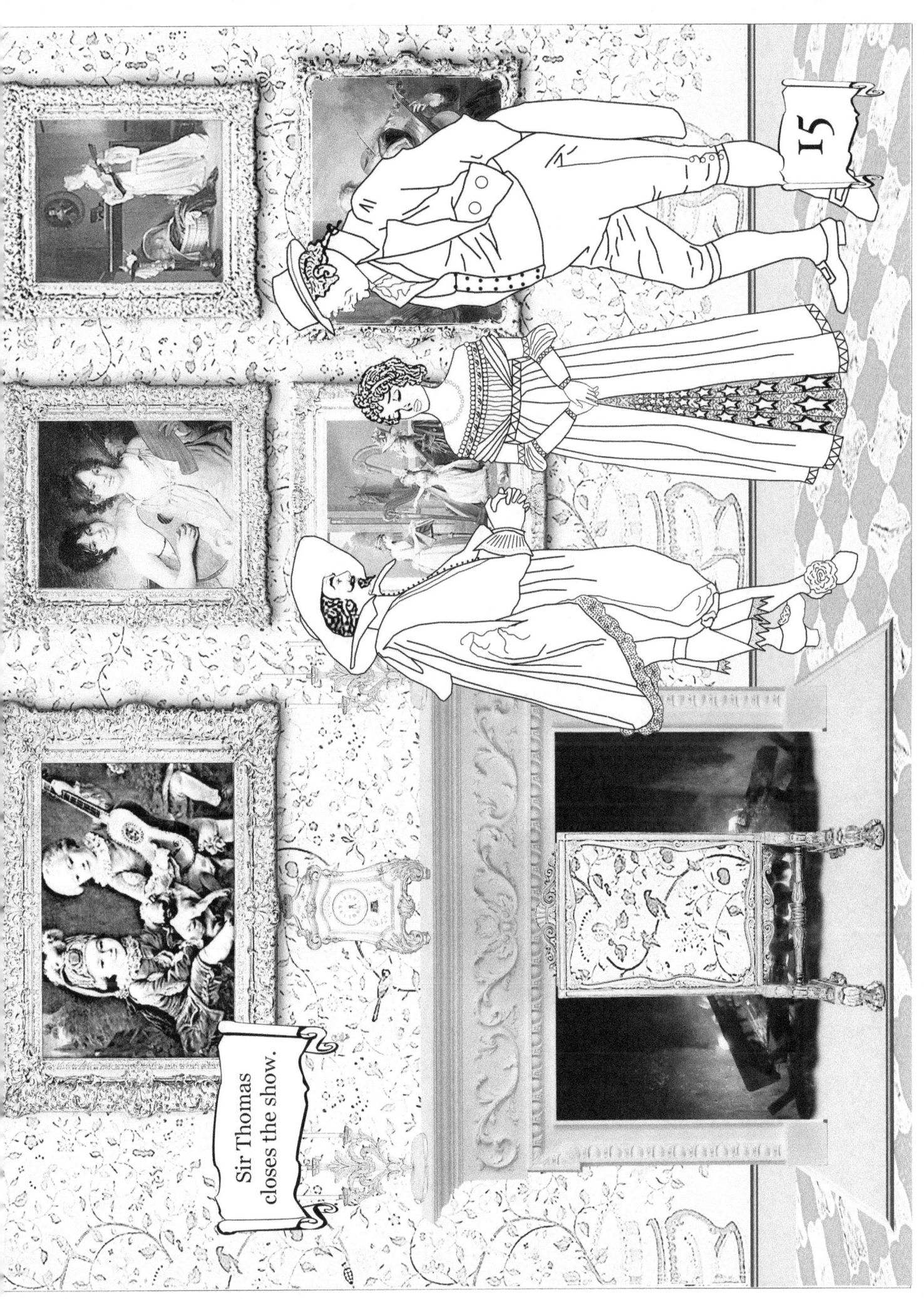

Sir Thomas closes the show.

15

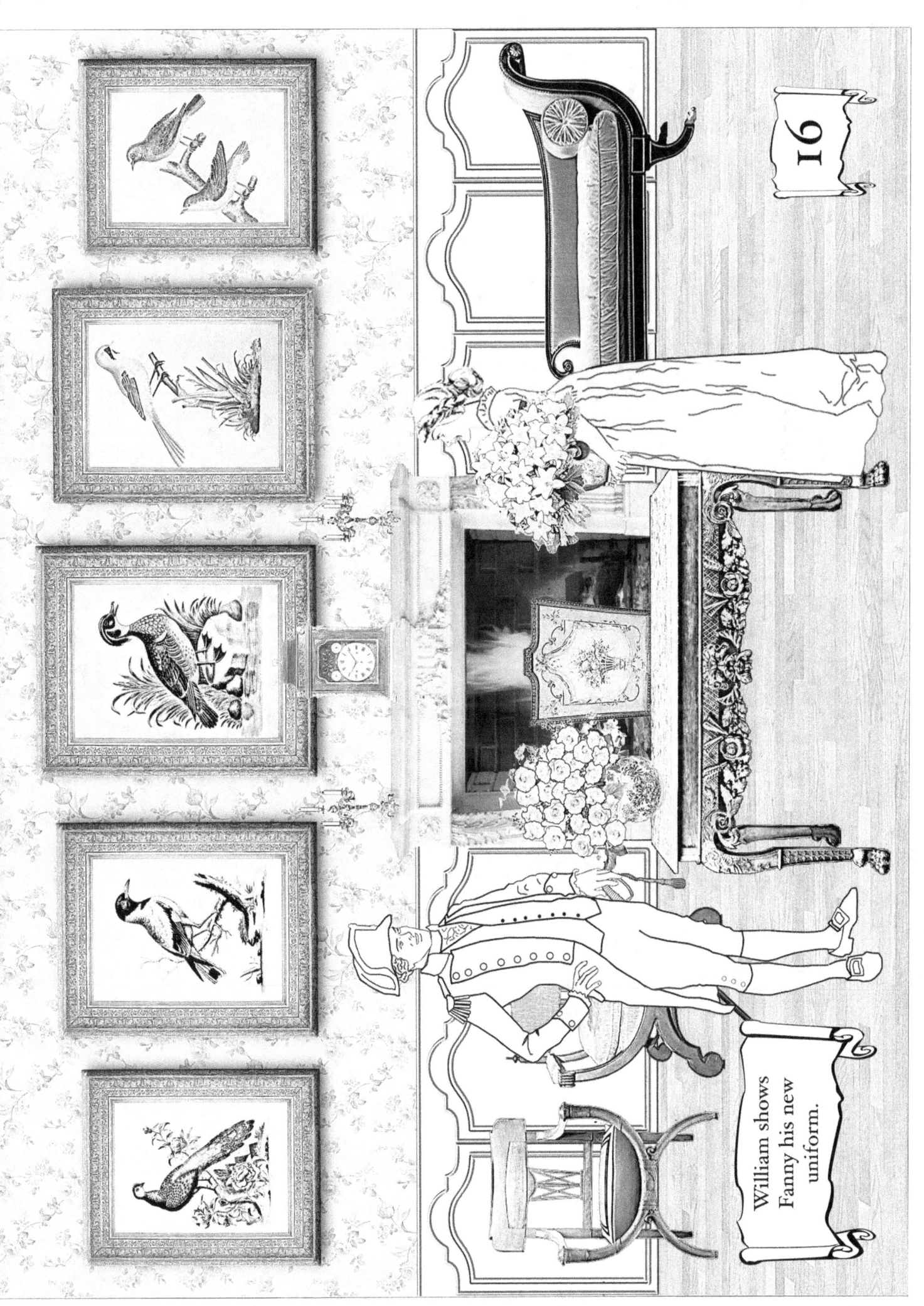

16

William shows
Fanny his new
uniform.

The wall is made up of ivory panels with gold trim.

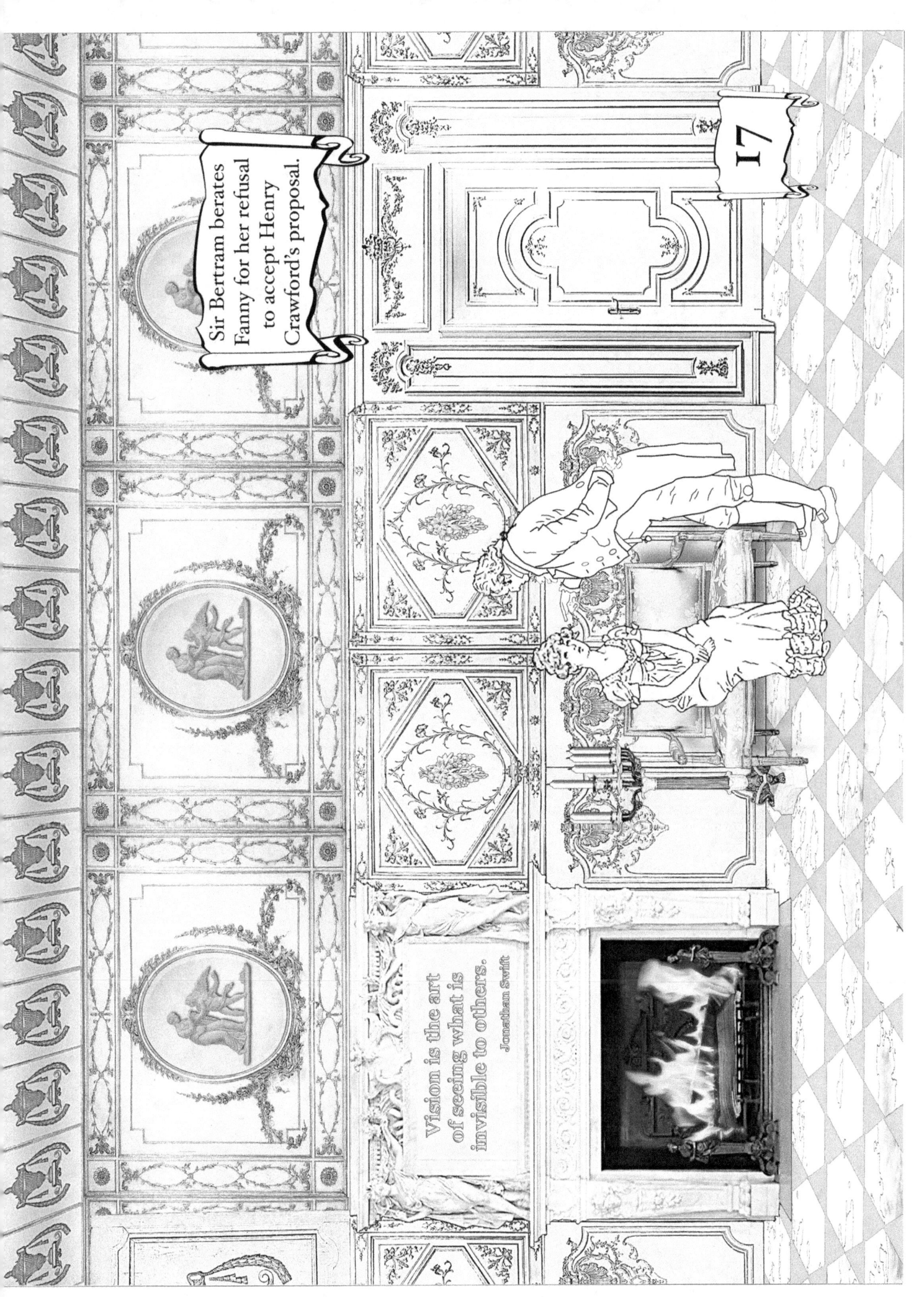

Sir Bertram berates Fanny for her refusal to accept Henry Crawford's proposal.

17

Vision is the art of seeing what is invisible to others.

Jonathan Swift

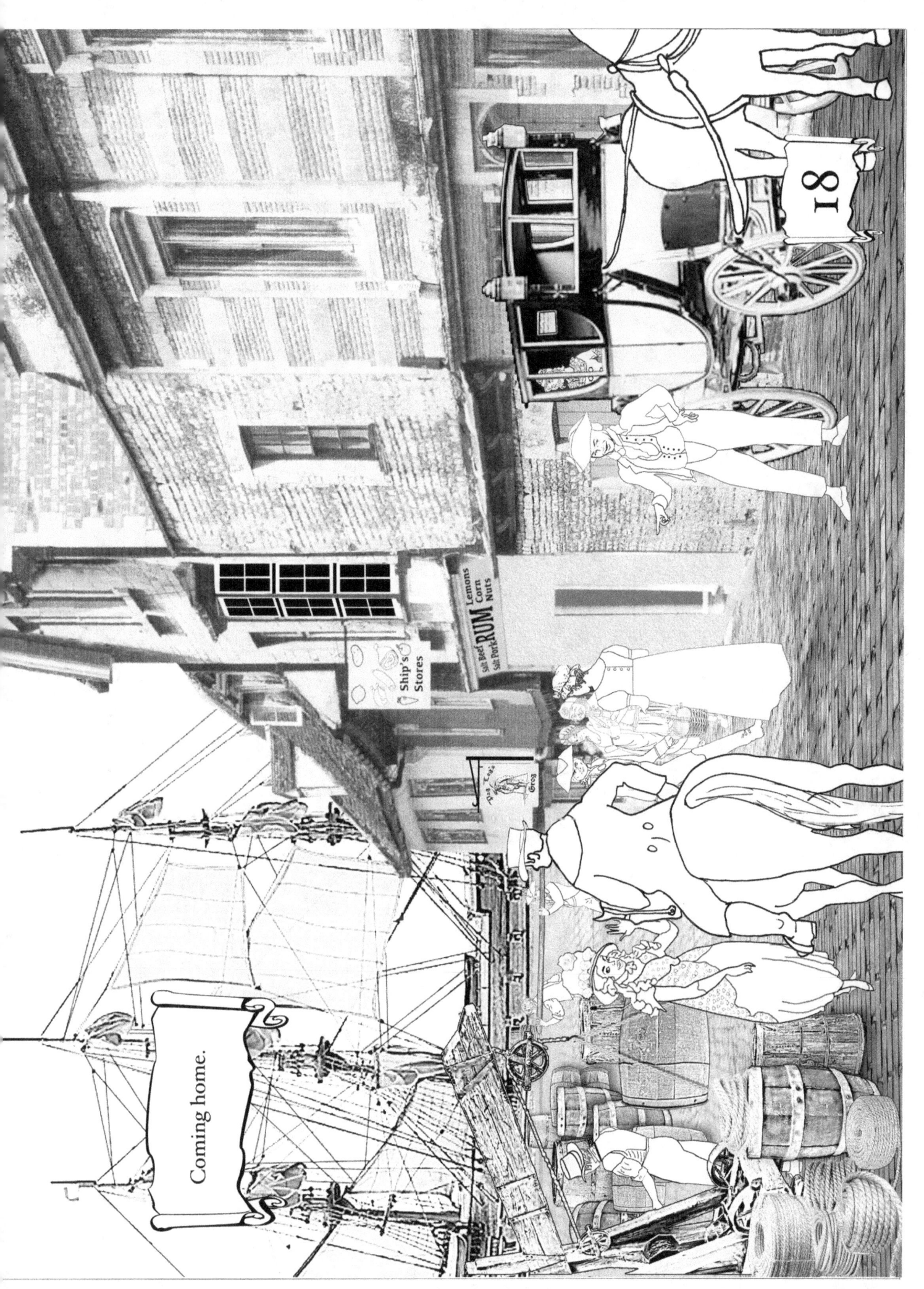

Coming home.

Ship's Stores

RUM
Lemons
Corn
Nuts
Salt Beef
Salt Pork

18

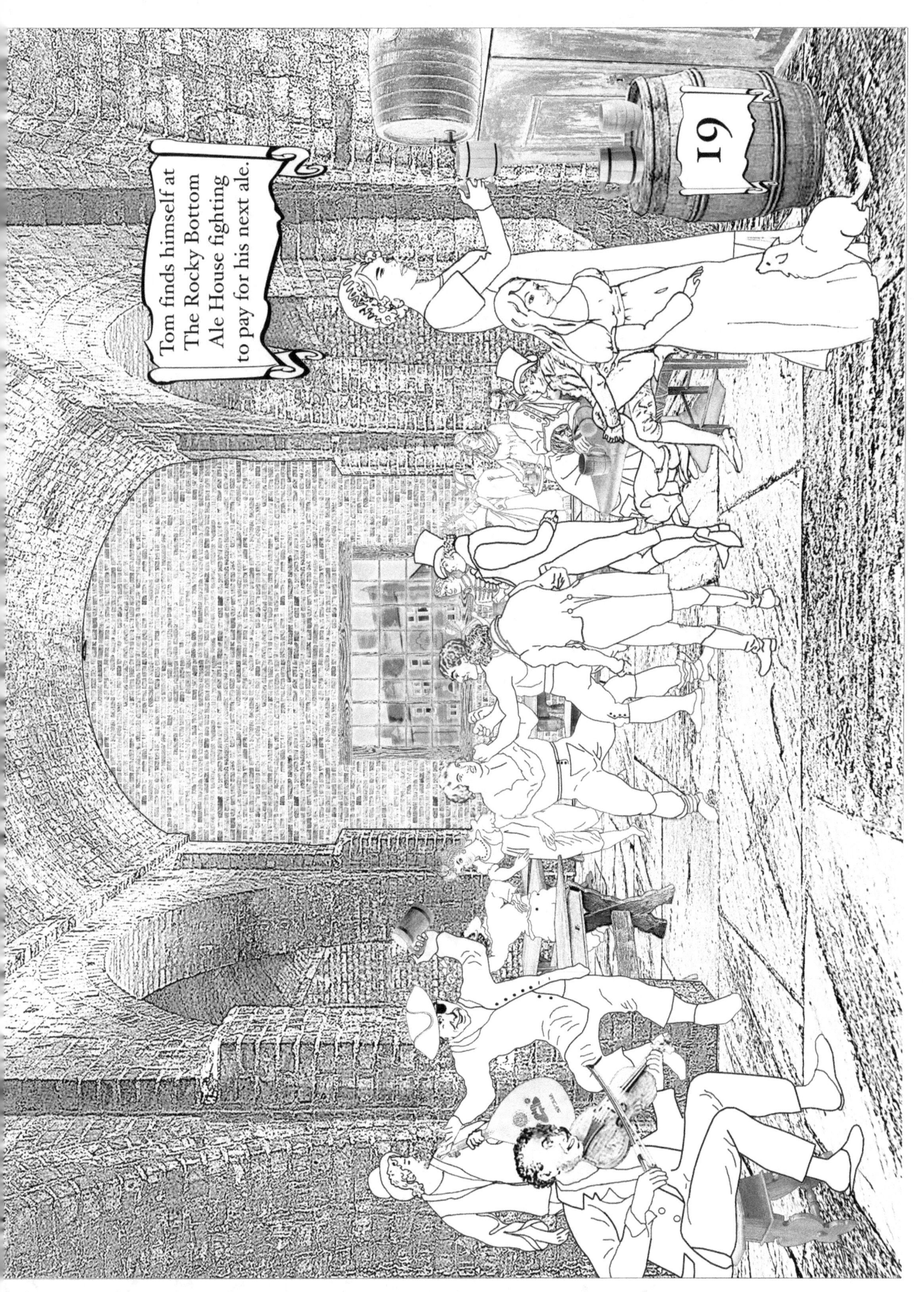

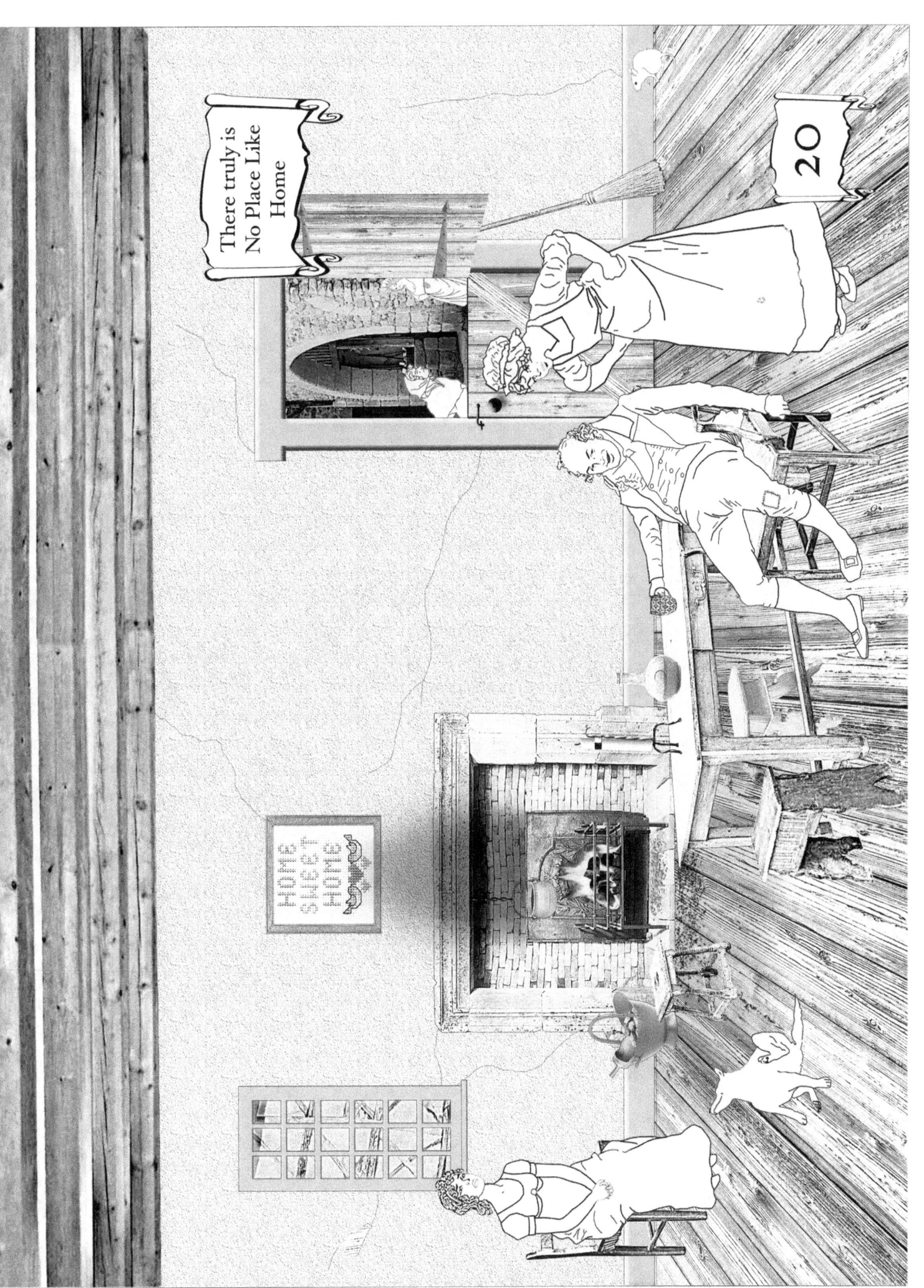

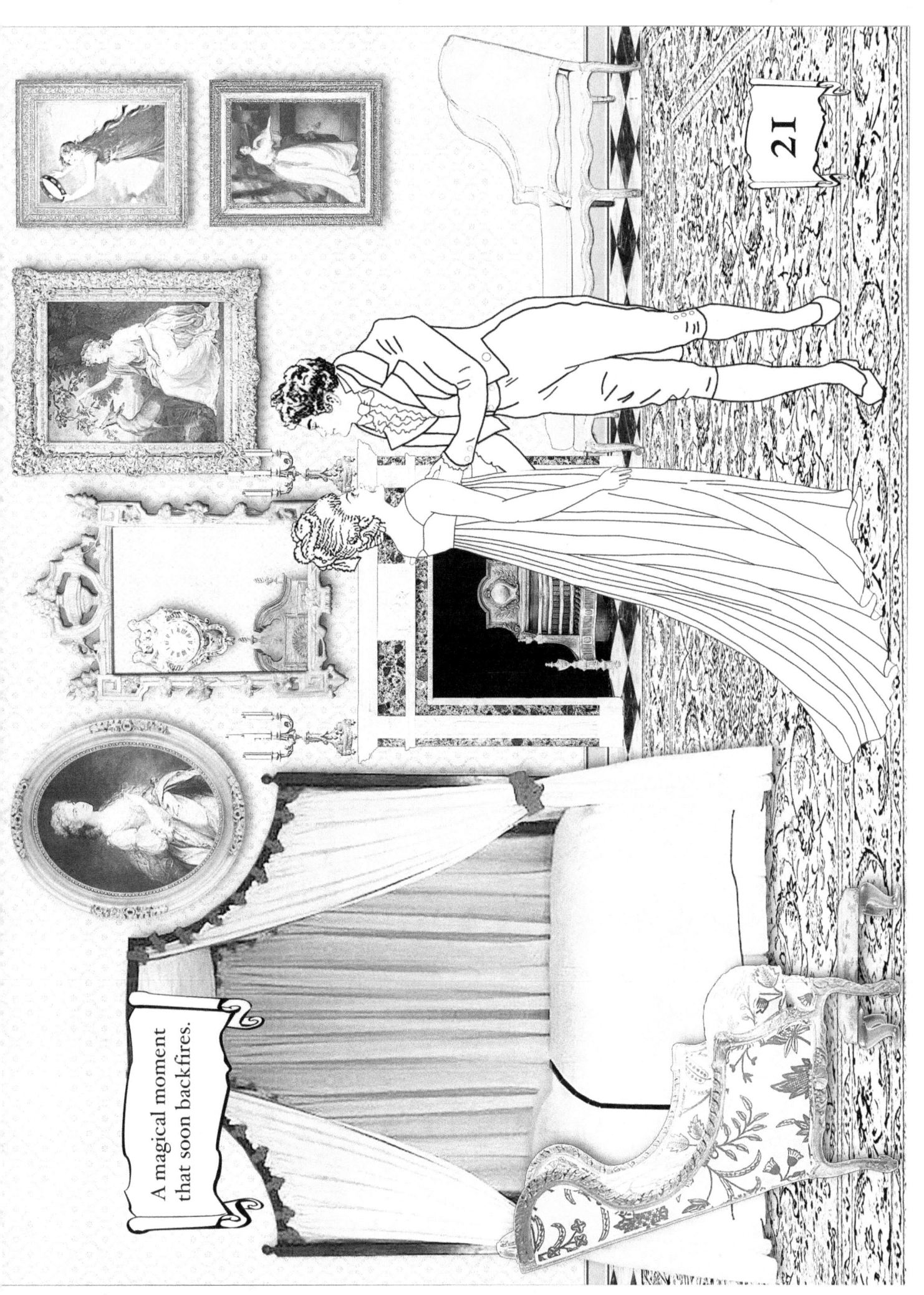

A magical moment that soon backfires.

21

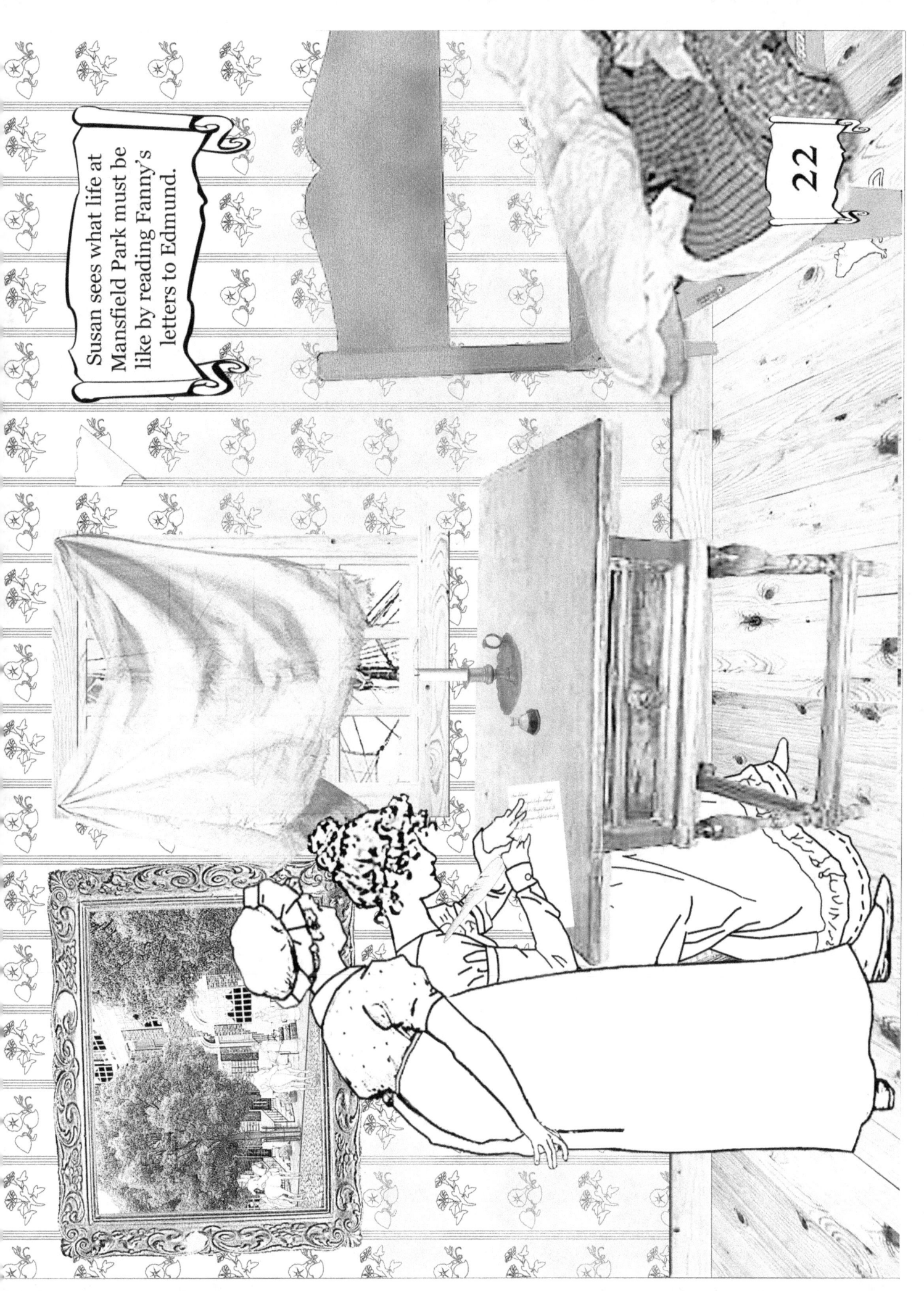

Susan sees what life at Mansfield Park must be like by reading Fanny's letters to Edmund.

22

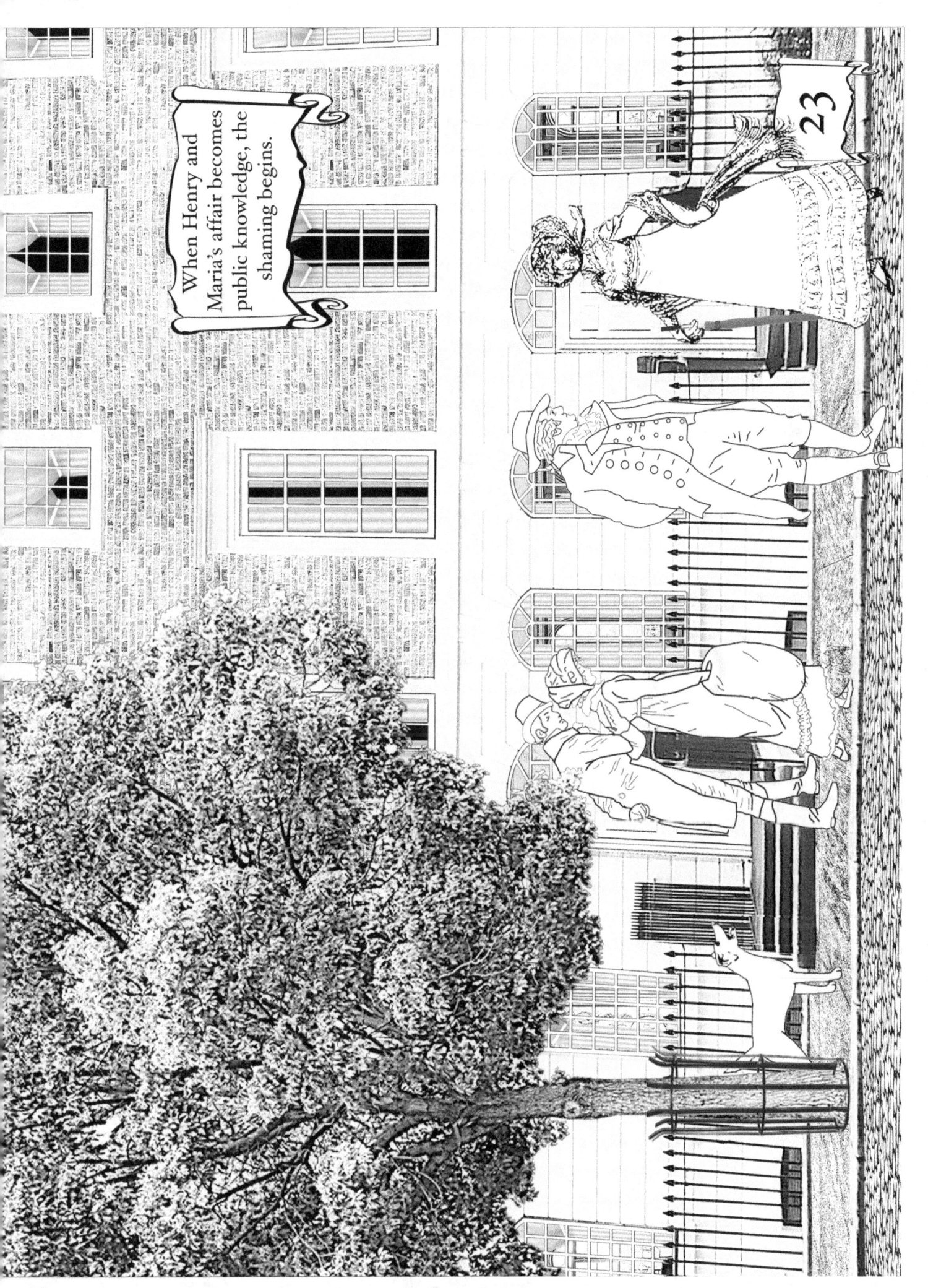

When Henry and Maria's affair becomes public knowledge, the shaming begins.

23

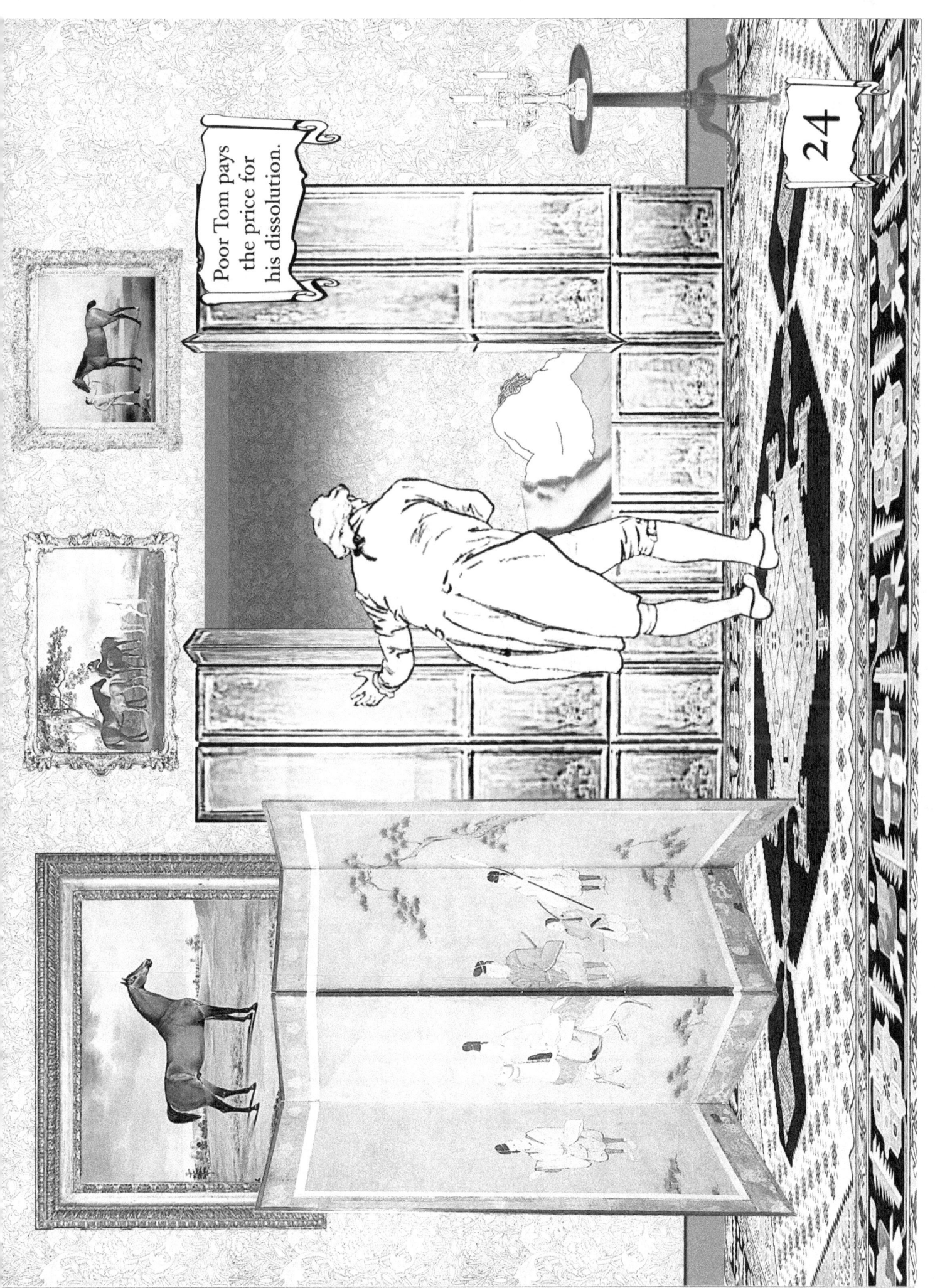

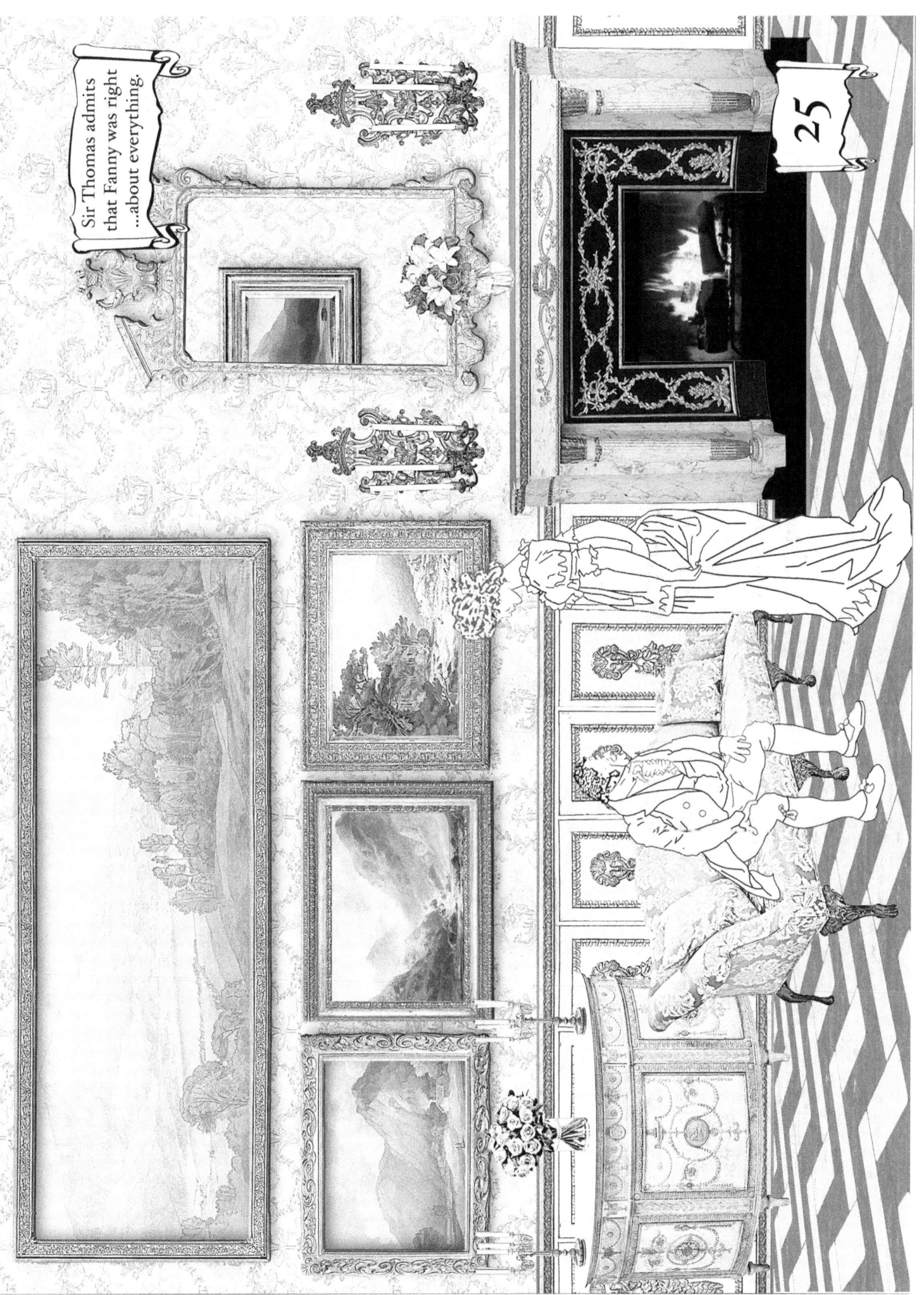

Sir Thomas admits that Fanny was right ...about everything.

25

England is dotted with the ruins of Catholic churches that were abandonded during the reign of King Henry VIII. He wanted to have his marriage to Catherine of Aragon annulled but the Pope wouldn't let him. Their feud led to the English Reformation and to those churches being turned into quarries for what followed them.

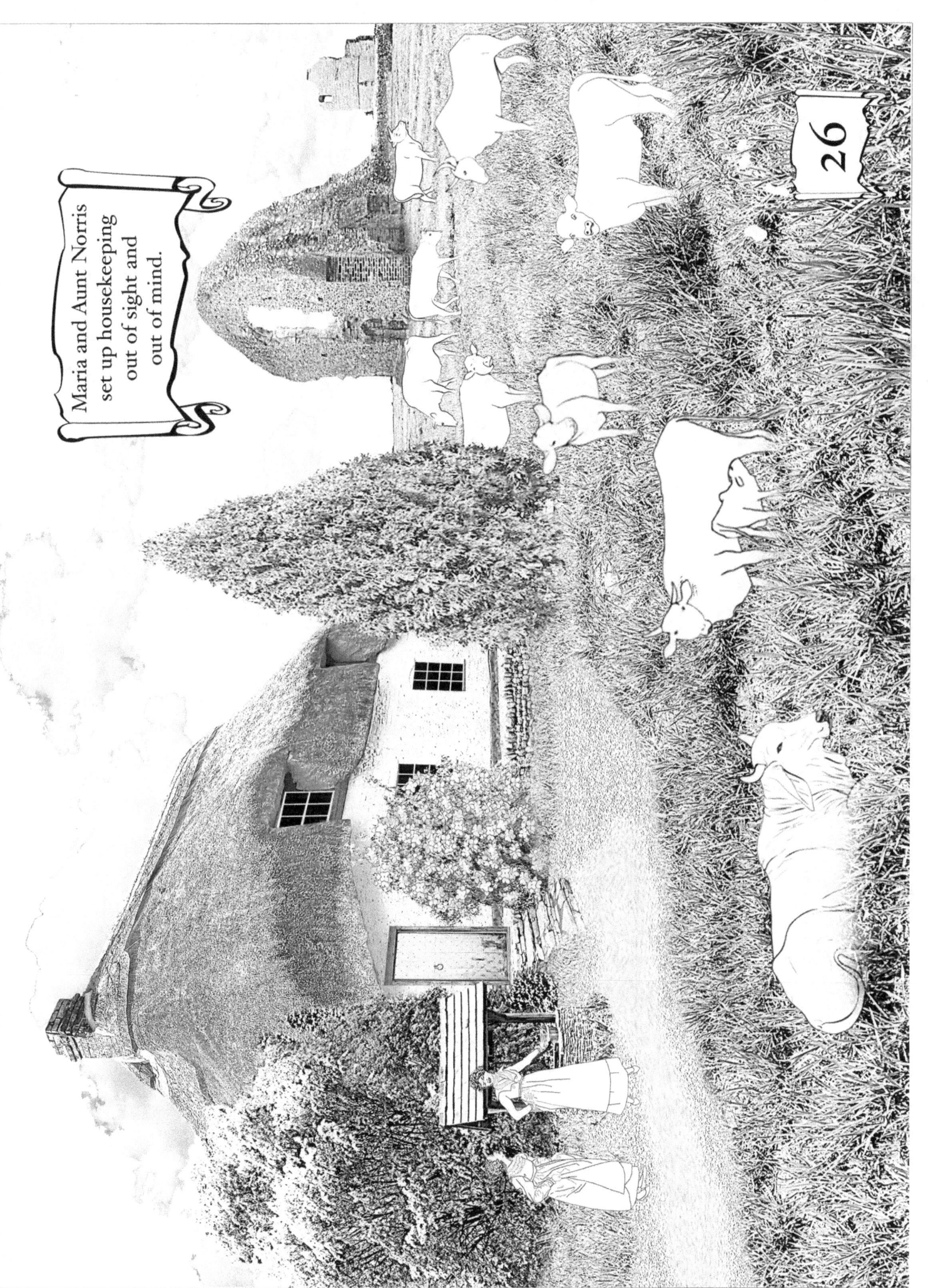

Maria and Aunt Norris set up housekeeping out of sight and out of mind.

26

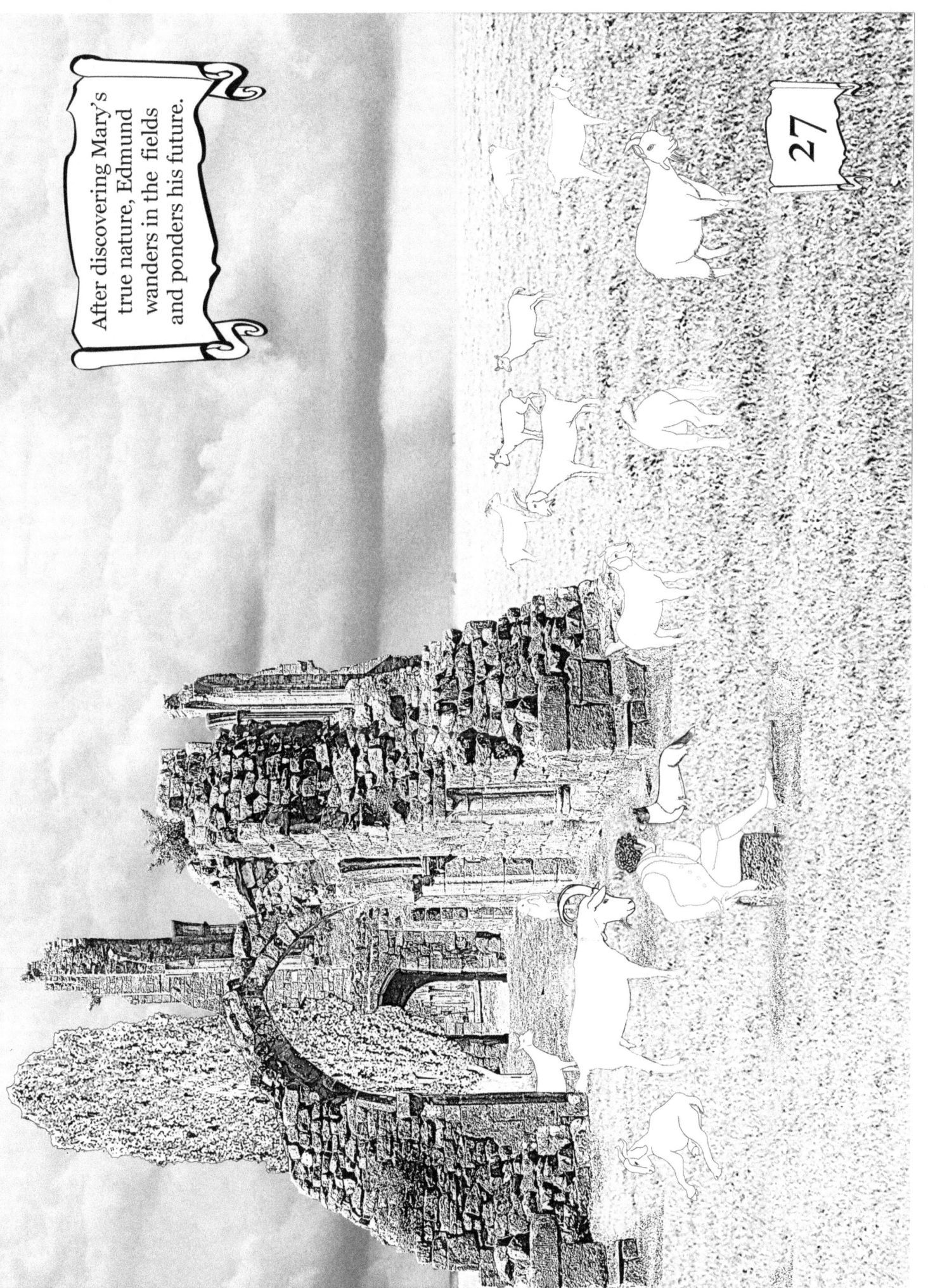

After discovering Mary's true nature, Edmund wanders in the fields and ponders his future.

27

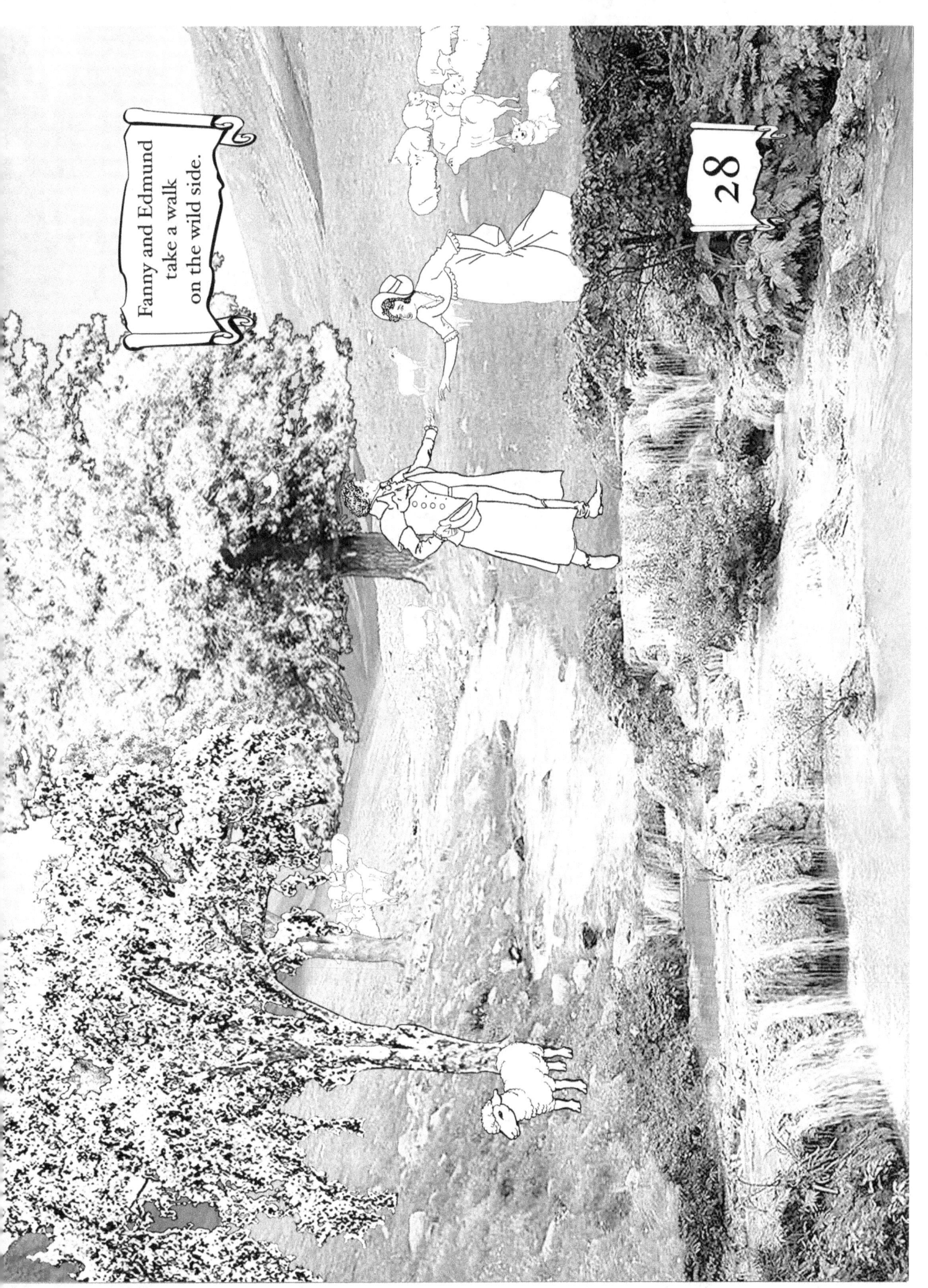

Fanny and Edmund take a walk on the wild side.

28

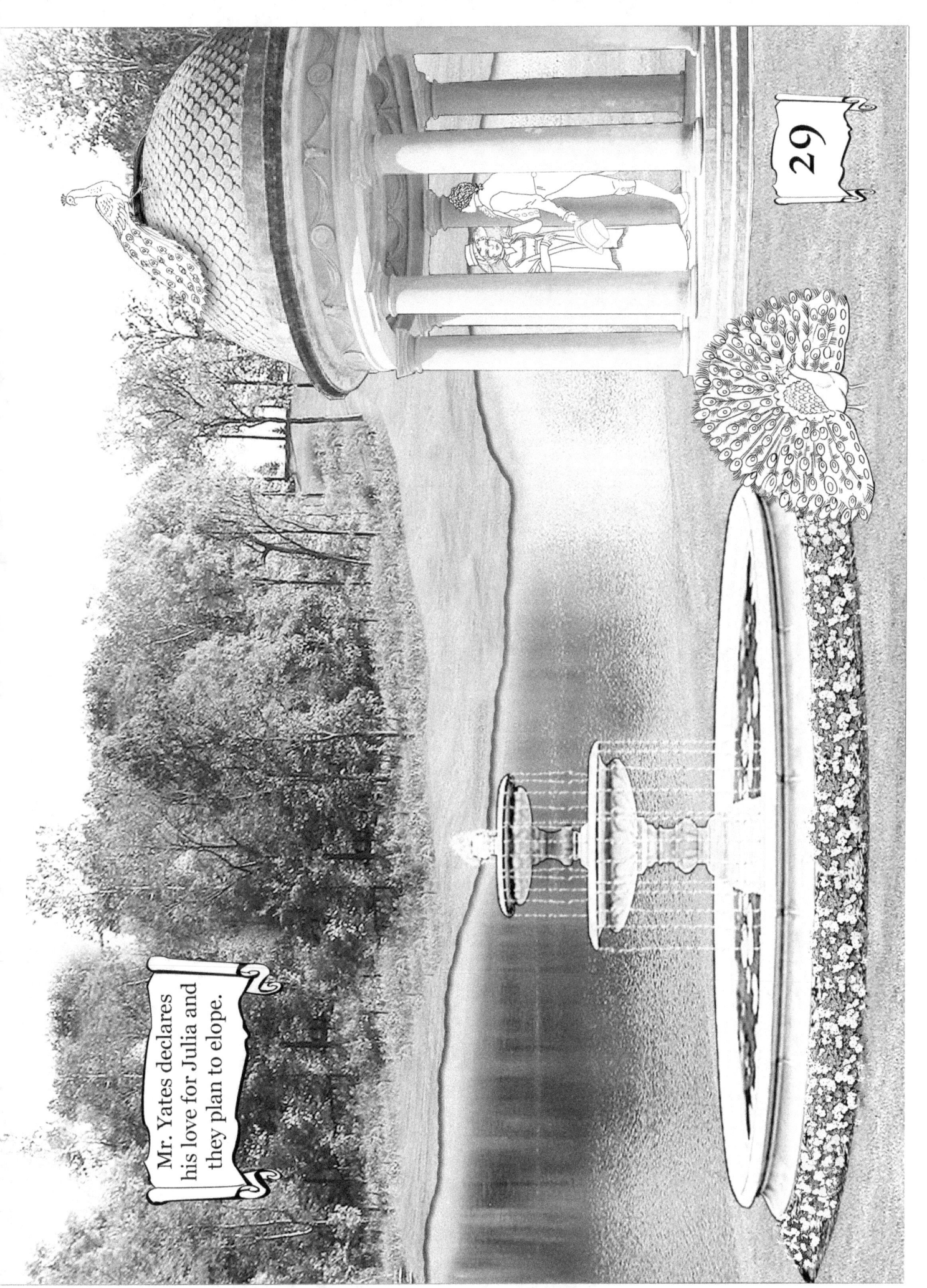

Mr. Yates declares his love for Julia and they plan to elope.

29

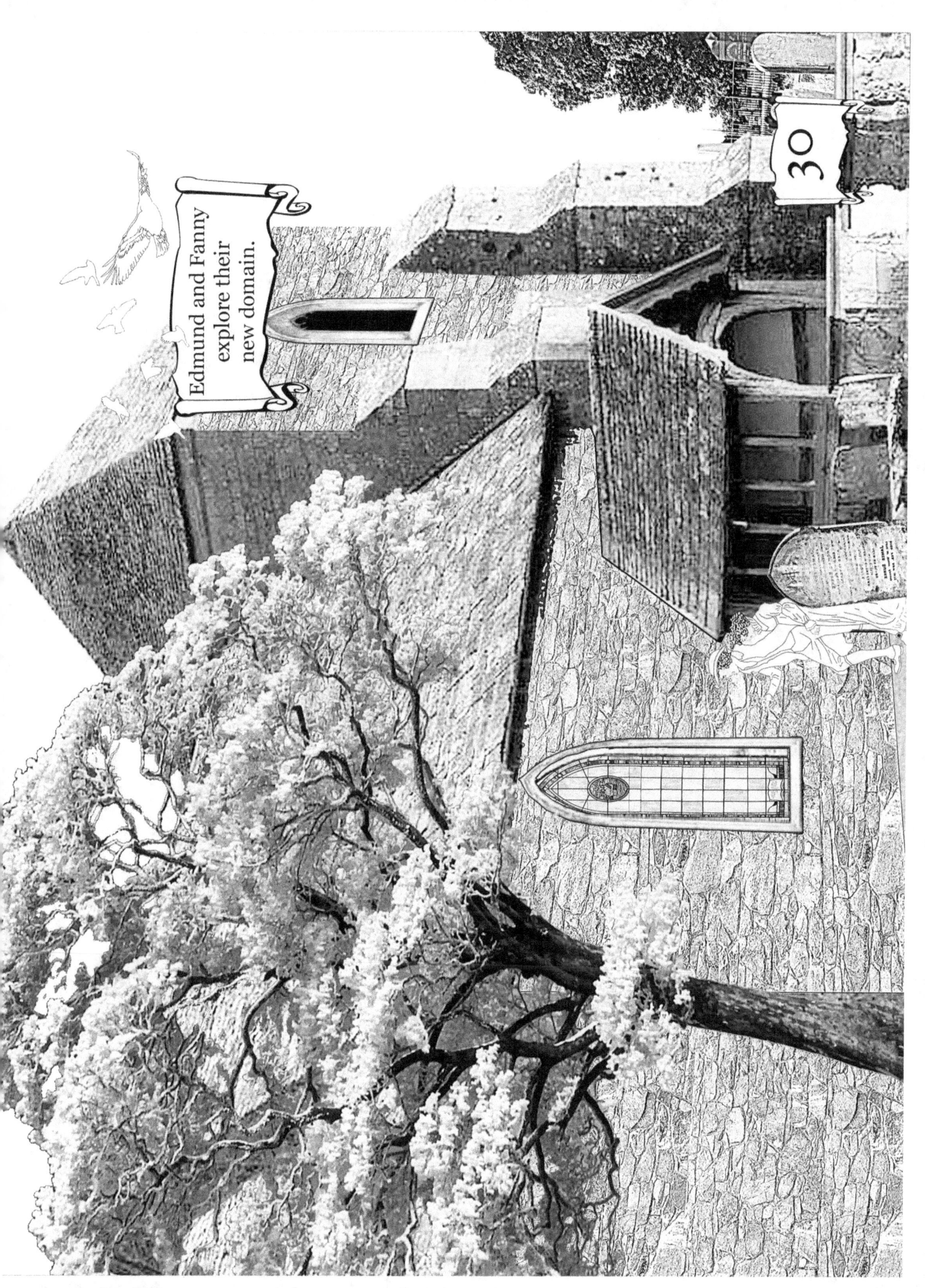

Edmund and Fanny explore their new domain.

30

www.ingramcontent.com/pod-product-compliance
Lightning Source LLC
Chambersburg PA
CBHW081618220526
45468CB00010B/2933